SECOND EDITION  3

Andrea DeHoyos
to perservere
perserverance
to keep trying: don't give
generous

Weaving It Together

Together

Connecting Reading and Writing

MILADA BROUKAL

D0139243

 THOMSON
HEINLE

Australia · Canada · Mexico · Singapore · United Kingdom · United States

THOMSON

HEINLE

Weaving It Together: Connecting Reading and Writing,
Book 3/Second Edition
Milada Broukal

Publisher, Adult and Academic ESL: James W. Brown
Senior Acquisitions Editor: Sherrise Roehr
Sr. Developmental Editor: Ingrid Wisniewska
Sr. Production Editor: Maryellen Killeen
Sr. Marketing Manager: Charlotte Sturdy
Sr. Print Buyer: Mary Beth Hennebury
Editorial Assistant: Audra Longert
Contributing Writer (Video Activities): Barbara Gaffney

Project Manager: Lifland et al., Bookmakers
Compositor: Parkwood Composition
Photography Manager: Sheri Blaney
Photo Researcher: Susan Van Etten
Illustrator: Ashley Van Etten
Cover Designer: Rotunda Design/Gina Petti
Interior Designer: Carole Rollins
Printer: Transcontinental Printing

Printed in Canada
1 2 3 4 5 6 7 8 9 10   07 06 05 04 03

For more information contact Heinle, 25 Thomson Place, Boston, Massachusetts 02210 USA, or you can visit our Internet site at http://www.heinle.com

For permission to use material from this text or product contact us:
Tel   1-800-730-2214
Fax   1-800-730-2215
Web   www.thomsonrights.com

Library of Congress Cataloging-in-Publication Data

Broukal, Milada.
    Weaving it together: connecting reading and writing/Milada Broukal.
       p. cm.
    Includes bibliographical references.
    Contents: Bk. 3. Intermediate level
    ISBN 0-8384-4818-6
    1. English language—Textbooks for foreign speakers. I. Title.

PE1128 .B7154 2003
428.2'4—dc21   2002032930

Photo credits: Cover: (top) Bonnie Kamin/Index Stock Imagery; (bottom) Carl Rosenstein/Index Stock Imagery. p. 1: (left) © PhotoDisc/Getty Images; (top right) © Royalty-Free/CORBIS; (bottom right): © ChromaZone Images/Index Stock Imagery. p. 13: (left and right) © Ewing Galloway/Index Stock Imagery. p. 29: © Bruce Burkhardt/CORBIS. p. 30: © Douglas Peebles/CORBIS. p. 40: © Robert Holmes/CORBIS. p. 51: © Jim Arbogast/CORBIS. p. 52: © DiMaggio/Kalish/CORBIS. p. 67: © Tomas del Amo/Index Stock Imagery. p. 81: © Archivo Iconografico, S.A./CORBIS. p. 82: © Bettmann/CORBIS. p. 94: © Bettmann/CORBIS. p. 107: © Erich Lessing/Art Resource, NY. p. 108: (left) © James Layfayette/Index Stock Imagery; (right) © Cable Photo Systems/Index Stock Imagery. p. 121: (left) Carl/Joan Vanderschuit/Index Stock Imagery; (right) © IPS/Index Stock Imagery. p. 149: © Amet Jean Pierre/CORBIS SYGMA. p. 163: © Allen Russell/Index Stock Imagery. p. 164: © Tony Ruta/Index Stock Imagery. p. 177: © David Young-Wolff/PhotoEdit. p. 189: © IT STOCK INT'L/Index Stock Imagery. p. 190: (left) © Alinari/Art Resource, NY; (right) © Royalty-Free/CORBIS. p. 198: © Aneal Vohra/Index Stock Imagery.

Text credits: p. 199: "The Untouchable" by William March. Reprinted by permission of Harold Ober Associates Incorporated. Copyright 1940, 1941, 1942, 1943, 1944, 1950, 1955, 1960 by Merchants National Bank of Mobile, Mobile, Alabama. p. 191: "Languages" by Carl Sandburg. From Carl Sandburg, *Chicago Poems* (New York: Henry Holt and Company, 1916), p. 175. PS 3537 A618C5 1916 Robarts Library.

Brief Contents

Weaving It Together 3 Contents

To the Teacher

Rationale

Weaving It Together, Book 3, is the third in a four-book series that integrates reading and writing skills for students of English as a second or foreign language. The complete program includes the following:

Book 1—Beginning Level

Book 2—High Beginning Level

Book 3—Intermediate Level

Book 4—High Intermediate Level

The central premise of *Weaving It Together* is that reading and writing are interwoven and inextricable skills. Good readers write well; good writers read well. With this premise in mind, *Weaving It Together* has been developed to meet the following objectives:

1. To combine reading and writing through a comprehensive, systematic, and engaging process designed to integrate the two effectively.
2. To provide academically bound students with serious and engaging multicultural content.
3. To promote individualized and cooperative learning within moderate-to large-sized classes.

Over the past few years, a number of noted researchers in the field of second language acquisition have written about the serious need to integrate reading and writing instruction in both classroom practice and materials development. *Weaving It Together* is, in many ways, a response to this need.

Barbara Kroll (1993), for example, talks of teaching students to read like writers and write like readers. She notes: "It is only when a writer is able to cast himself or herself in the role of a reader of the text under preparation that he or she is able to anticipate the reader's needs by writing into the text what he or she expects or wants the reader to take out from the text." Through its systematic approach to integrating reading and writing, *Weaving It Together* teaches ESL and EFL students to understand the kinds of interconnections that they need to make between reading and writing in order to achieve academic success.

Linda Lonon Blanton's research (1992) focuses on the need for second language students to develop authority, conviction, and certainty in their writing. She believes that students develop strong writing skills in concert with good reading skills. Blanton writes: "My experience tells me that empowerment, or achieving this certainty and authority, can be achieved only through performance—through the act of speaking and writing about texts, through developing individual responses to texts." For Blanton, as for Kroll and others, both reading and writing must be treated as composing processes. Effective writing instruction must be integrally linked with effective reading instruction. This notion is at the heart of *Weaving It Together.*

Organization of the Text

Weaving It Together, Book 3, contains eight thematically organized units, each of which includes two interrelated chapters. Each chapter begins with a reading, moves on to a set of activities designed to develop critical reading skills, and culminates with a series of interactive writing exercises.
Each chapter contains the same sequence of activities:

1. **Pre-reading activity and predicting:** Each chapter is introduced with a picture, accompanied by a set of discussion questions and a predicting exercise. The purpose of the pre-reading activity is to prepare students for the reading by activating their background knowledge and encouraging them to call on and share their experiences. The purpose of the predicting activity is to prepare students for the ideas and vocabulary in the reading. This will make the reading easier to understand and help students to integrate the new information in the text with their existing ideas.

2. **Reading:** Each reading is a high-interest passage related to the theme of the unit. Selected topics include colors, alternative medicine, and changes in the English language. The final unit includes readings from literature.

3. **Vocabulary:** The vocabulary in bold type in each reading passage is practiced in the vocabulary exercises that follow the passage. There are two types of vocabulary exercises. The first one, *Meaning,* uses the new words in the context in which they were used in the reading. The second one, *Word Building,* helps students to develop word-building skills, giving them greater flexibility in the use of these words when they are writing their own essays on the same theme.

4. **Comprehension:** There are two types of comprehension exercises: The first, *Looking for Main Ideas,* concentrates on a general understanding of the reading. This exercise may be done after a first

silent reading of the text. Students can reread the text to check answers. The second comprehension exercise, *Looking for Details*, concentrates on developing skimming and scanning skills.

5. **Discussion:** Working in small or large groups, students are encouraged to interact with one another to discuss questions that arise from the reading. The discussion questions ask students to relate their experiences to what they have learned from the reading. The questions in the discussion section can provide information on one of the topics to be written on in the writing practice section.

6. **Model essay:** Each unit contains an essay written by an international student whose writing skills are slightly more advanced than those of the writers who will use *Weaving It Together, Book 3.* The essay follows the general rhetorical form of North American academic prose and provides natural preparation for the discrete points taught in the organizing section.

7. **Organizing:** In connection with each of the sixteen readings, a different aspect of essay writing is developed. These aspects include essay organization, structure, transitions, and rhetorical devices the students may use to develop their own essays. Exercises following the instructional text reinforce the organizational techniques introduced.

8. **Writing practice:** Three different brainstorming techniques are presented on pages 208–211. Before students begin writing their outline, you may want to refer them to these pages to try out and practice a variety of brainstorming techniques that will help them to activate their background knowledge. Using the ideas they have generated in the pre-writing stage, students next put together an outline for their writing. This outline acts as a framework for the work ahead. The next step is to write a rough draft of the essay. *Weaving It Together* encourages students to write several drafts, since writing is an ongoing process. Students can then work on their own or with a partner to check their essays, making any necessary alterations. Teachers are encouraged to add to the checklist provided any further points they consider important. Next, students are encouraged to work with a partner or their teacher to correct spelling, punctuation, vocabulary, and grammar. Finally, students prepare the final version of the essay.

Optional Expansion Activities

1. **Quiz:** At the end of each unit is a fun quiz related to the theme of the unit. The answers appear at the end of the book. The quiz questions are meant to be a light-hearted way to end the unit. Use them

as a team competition or as a game. Students can also make up further quiz questions to test each other.

2. **Video activity:** Following the quiz is a video activity related to the CNN videotapes that accompany this series. The video activity can be used to expand vocabulary and themes in the unit. Each video activity ends with a discussion question, which can be used as a springboard for further writing.

3. **Internet activity:** Also at the end of each unit is an Internet activity, which gives students the opportunity to develop their Internet research skills. This activity may be done in a classroom setting, under the guidance of the teacher, or—if students have Internet access—as a homework task leading to a classroom presentation or discussion. Each Internet activity has two parts. The first part involves doing some research on the Internet using the key words suggested. The second part involves evaluating web sites in order to assess the reliability of the information they contain.

Journal Writing

In addition to doing the projects and exercises in the book, I strongly recommend that students be instructed to keep a journal in which they correspond with you. The purpose of this journal is for them to tell you how they feel about the class each day. It gives them an opportunity to tell you what they like, what they dislike, what they understand, and what they don't understand. By having students explain what they have learned in the class, you can discover whether they understand the concepts taught.

Journal writing is effective for two major reasons. First, because this type of writing focuses on fluency and personal expression, students always have something to write about. Second, journal writing can be used to identify language concerns and trouble spots that need further review. In its finest form, journal writing becomes an active dialogue between teacher and student that permits you to learn more about your students' lives and to individualize their language instruction.

References

Blanton, Linda Lonon. 1992. "Reading, Writing, and Authority: Issues in Developmental ESL." *College ESL,* 2, 11–19.

Kroll, Barbara. 1993. "Teaching Writing *Is* Teaching Reading: Training the New Teacher of ESL Composition." In *Reading in the Composition Classroom.* Boston: Heinle & Heinle Publishers, pp. 61–81.

To the Student

This book will teach you to read and write in English. You will study readings on selected themes and learn strategies for writing good sentences on those themes. In the process, you will be exposed to the writings and ideas of others, as well as to ways of expressing your own ideas so that you can work toward writing an essay of four or five paragraphs in good English.

It is important for you to know that writing well in English may be quite different from writing well in your native language. Good Chinese, Arabic, or Spanish writing is different from good English writing. Not only are the styles different, but the organization is different too.

The processes of reading and writing are closely interconnected. Therefore, in this book, we are weaving reading and writing together. I hope that the readings in the book will stimulate your interest to write and that *Weaving It Together* will make writing in English much easier for you.

Note for the New Edition

In this new edition of *Weaving It Together, Book 3*, I have added extra exercises on predicting and word-building. There is a new unit on the topic of the environment and a new unit with readings from literature. For those of you who enjoy using different media, I have also added CNN video and Internet activities. I hope that you will enjoy using these new features and that *Weaving It Together* will continue to help you toward success.

Symbols

CHAPTER ONE

Color Me Pink

Pre-Reading Activity

Discuss these questions.

1. Imagine yourself as the person in the picture. How would you feel if the room were all blue? *groomi*
2. How would you feel if the room were all red?
3. How would you feel if the room were all black?
4. What color would you like this room to be?

Predicting

What feeling do you associate with each of these colors? Match each color with a feeling. Then compare your ideas with those in the reading.

1. *Peace* blue
2. *a* red
3. *Kindness* green
4. *corage* yellow
5. *e* brown
6. *wealth* pink

a. energy *red* ✓
b. kindness *pink*
c. wealth *Brown* x
d. courage *yellow* ✓
e. sadness *blue* x
f. peace *pink* x *green*

Color Me Pink

Red, white, pink, purple—what is your favorite color? We are all sensitive to color. There are some colors we like a lot and some we don't like at all. Some colors **soothe** us, others excite us, some make us happy, and others make us sad. People are affected by color more than they realize because color is tied to all aspects of our lives.

Experts in colorgenics, the study of the language of color, believe that the colors we wear say a lot about us. Do you know why you select a shirt or dress of a certain color when you look through your clothes in the morning? Colorgenics experts say that we **subconsciously** choose to wear certain colors in order to communicate our desires, emotions, and needs.

Colorgenics experts claim that our clothes send messages to others about our mood, personality, and desires. For these experts, pink expresses the peace and **contentment** of the wearer. People who often wear pink are supposed to be warm and understanding. The message is that you would like to share your peace and happiness with others. Red garments, on the other hand, indicate a high level of physical energy. People who wear red like to take life at a fast **pace.** Brown is the color of wealth, and it shows a need for independence and material security. Wearers of green have a love of nature and enjoy peaceful moments. They often like to be left alone with their thoughts.

Although colorgenics may be a recent area of study, associating colors with emotions is not new. Colors have always been used to describe not only our feelings but also our physical health and attitudes. "Red with rage" describes anger; "in the pink" means to be in good health; "feeling blue" is a sad way to feel; and "green with envy" indicates a jealous **attitude.**

Color is used symbolically in all cultures, and it plays an important role in ceremonies and festivities. Yellow is a symbol of luck in Peru, and it can be seen just about everywhere during New Year celebrations—in flowers, clothing, and decorations. Some Peruvians say, "The more yellow you have around you, the luckier you will be in the new year." Yellow is also an important color to the Vietnamese, who use it at weddings and also on their flag, where it represents courage, victory, and sacrifice. In many cultures, white symbolizes purity, which is why brides often wear white wedding gowns. Black, on the other hand, symbolizes death, and it is often the color people wear to funerals.

According to colorgenics experts, colors not only are a mirror of ourselves, but have an effect on us as well. Blue is calming, while red is **stimulating** and exciting. It's no **coincidence** that racing cars are often painted red. Yellow is a happy color that makes us feel good about life. Pink awakens love and kindness.

Some experts are so convinced that colors have a strong effect on us that they believe colors can be used to heal. They say that by concentrating our thoughts on certain colors, we can cause energy to go to the parts of the body that need treatment. White light is said to be cleansing, and it can balance the body's entire system. Yellow stimulates the mind and creates a positive attitude, so it can help against depression. Green, which has a calming and restful effect, is supposed to be good for heart conditions. Books are now available that teach people how to heal with color. These books provide long lists of **ailments** and the colors that can heal them.

Some psychologists and physicians also use color to help them treat patients with emotional and psychological problems. By giving patients what is called the Luscher color test, in which they select the colors they like and dislike, doctors can learn many things about patients' personalities.

In conclusion, the study of color can help us to understand ourselves and to improve our lives. It offers an alternative way to heal the body and spirit, and it can help us understand what others are trying to communicate. We can then respond to their needs and achieve a new level of understanding.

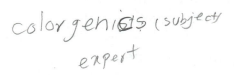

colorgenics (subject
expert

Vocabulary

[handwritten: every thing will be okey meaning work Building]
[handwritten: don't worry]

Meaning

[handwritten: relax, calm dawn, you'll be okey]

Complete each definition with one of the following words.

soothe	coincidence	pace
attitude	ailments	contentment
stimulating	subconsciously	

1. People who are sick have ___ailment___.

2. To ___soothe___ someone is to comfort the person and make the person feel better.

3. Something that excites us and makes us active is ___stimulatling___.

4. To do something _____ is to act without actively knowing that you are doing it.

5. When things happen by ___coincidace___ *[handwritten: telephone]*, they appear to be connected in some way but really are not.

6. Your ___attitudl___ is the feeling or emotion you have toward something.
   [handwritten: good attitude / bad attitude]

7. To be happy and at ease is to feel ___contentment___ *[handwritten: ₌ satisfuy]*

8. ___Pace___ is the speed at which we do things.

Word Building

[handwritten Arabic text] I am content

Complete the sentences with the correct form of the word in capital letters. You may use your dictionary. The first one is done as an example.

[handwritten: I am content with this course]

1. SYMBOL
   a. The color red <u>symbolizes</u> anger.
   b. Colors are used <u>symbolically</u> to express feelings.

[handwritten: what do you find stimulating]

2. EMOTION
    a. People react _Emotionally_ to different colors.
    b. You can express your _emotions_ by wearing different colors.

3. PSYCHOLOGY
    a. Some _psychologist_ use color to treat patients.
    b. Colors can help people with _psychological_ problems.

Comprehension

Looking for the Main Ideas

Circle the letter of the correct answer.

1. Learning about color can help us to _____.
    a. express our ideas more clearly
    b. control our desires
    c. understand ourselves and others
    d. feel happier

2. Colors _____.
    a. have similar meanings around the world
    b. are not often used in a symbolic way
    c. say something about our personality
    d. are used to influence others

3. Some experts believe that _____.
    a. colors can be used to heal
    b. associating colors with emotions is something new
    c. most colors have a calming effect on us
    d. colors can influence our personality

Looking for Details

Scan the reading quickly to find the answers to these questions. Write complete sentences.

1. What do colorgenics experts say about a person who likes to wear pink?

   They are supposed to be warm and understanding

2. What does white symbolize in many cultures?

   Purity (n) pure (w) clean innocent

3. What is yellow a symbol of in Peru?

   luck

4. According to colorgenics experts, how does red make us feel?

   energetic

   It is stimulating, gets your energy up

5. According to colorgenics experts, how does blue make us feel?

6. According to some experts, green is a color for healing. What part of the body do they think it is good for?

   heart conditions

7. What is the name of the test some psychologists use to help them treat their patients?

   luscher color test

Making Inferences and Drawing Conclusions

The answers to these questions are not directly stated in the reading. Write complete answers.

1. Why might it be good for a decorator to study colorgenics?

   _____

   _____

2. Why is color an important part of ceremonies and festivities?

   _____

   _____

3. How might the Luscher color test help a psychologist treat a patient?

   _____

   _____

4. How might learning about color be useful in our lives?

   _____

   _____

5. What colors would you use in (a) a child's bedroom and (b) a classroom?

   _____

   _____

Discussion

Discuss these questions with your classmates.

1. What colors are you wearing today? Do you think they are a reflection of your feelings?
2. Look at the colors your classmates are wearing. Do you think the colors they are wearing match their personalities?
3. Do some colors make you feel better than others?
4. What do you like or dislike about the way colors are used in your environment?
5. What colors are symbolic in your culture?

Organizing

A paragraph is a basic unit of organization for writing a group of sentences that develop one main idea. There are three parts to a paragraph:

1. A topic sentence
2. Supporting sentences
3. A concluding sentence

The Topic Sentence

The *topic sentence* is the most important sentence in the paragraph. It is the main idea of the paragraph. The topic sentence controls and limits the ideas that can be discussed in a paragraph.

The topic sentence has two parts: the topic and the controlling idea. The *topic* is the subject of the paragraph.

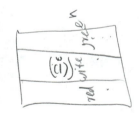

Example:

The color yellow is the color of mental activity.
Topic: The color yellow

The *controlling idea* limits or controls your topic to one aspect that you want to write about.

Examples:

<u>Brown</u> is the color of <u>material security</u>.
(Topic)   (Controlling idea)

or

<u>Brown</u> shows <u>a desire for stability</u>.
(Topic)   (Controlling idea)

A topic can have more than one controlling idea. You could write one paragraph about the color brown indicating material security and another on the desire for stability.

Circle the topic and underline the controlling idea in each of these topic sentences.

1. The colors we wear change our emotions.

2. People who wear orange like to communicate with others.

3. People who wear red clothes want to have fun.

4. Shoes give us lots of information about the person wearing them.

5. Patterns on clothing give us clues to the mood of the wearer.

6. People who wear yellow are often creative.

7. Turquoise is good for people who have decisions to make.

8. People who wear green often like the outdoors.

Supporting Sentences

Supporting sentences develop the topic sentence. They give the reader reasons, examples, and more facts about the topic sentence. They must all be related to the topic sentence.

Exercise 2

Look at the underlined topic sentences. In each case, one of the sentences below it does not support the topic sentence. Circle the letter of your answer.

1. Colors are often divided into two groups, warm and cold.
   a. The warm colors are red, pink, yellow, and orange.
   b. These colors are associated with activity and energy.
   c. Violet is the color of royalty and is often worn by political and religious leaders.
   d. The cold colors—blue, purple, violet, and brown—are calm and mysterious.

2. <u>Socks and stockings give us clues to a person's inner personality.</u>
   - a. Socks and stockings are available in more colors now than ever before.
   - b. Red socks show that the wearer has lots of energy that he or she needs to let go of.
   - c. Wearers of white socks and stockings are often hiding their true feelings.
   - d. Green socks are worn when a person feels the need for rest and relaxation.

3. <u>The Luscher color test is made up of eight colors that have been carefully chosen for their meanings.</u>
   - a. Dr. Max Luscher, the inventor of the test, was born in Basel, Switzerland, in 1923.
   - b. Each of the eight colors has the same meaning and importance the world over.
   - c. The colors in the test are gray, blue, green, red, yellow, violet, brown, and black.
   - d. The colors indicate what kind of personality you have.

4. <u>Colors are symbolic and have many different meanings to people around the world.</u>
   - a. In America, red, white, and blue, the colors of the flag, symbolize patriotism.
   - b. Green is a sign of birth and new life to the Irish.
   - c. Blue looks good on people with blue eyes.
   - d. Some colors represent male and female, such as pink and blue.

The Concluding Sentence

The last sentence of your paragraph is called the *concluding sentence.* This sentence signals the end of the paragraph.

The concluding sentence is similar to the topic sentence. Both are general sentences. The concluding sentence can be written in two ways:

1. State the topic sentence in *different* words.

   or

2. Summarize the main points in the paragraph.

Begin a concluding sentence with one of these phrases:

In conclusion, . . .

or

In summary, . . .

Write a topic sentence for each of these paragraphs.

1. *Topic Sentence:* _____

   _____

   If your favorite color is white, you are probably very moral and sometimes have old-fashioned ideas about romance. People who like red, on the other hand, want excitement, variety, and change and are often more interested in passion than true love. Pink lovers are warm and understanding people who believe in loyalty and make good mates. Those who like the color blue are emotional and romantic and need lots of attention from their partners.

2. *Topic Sentence:* _____

   _____

   Violet is a color that affects the bones in the body and can be used to heal the pain of arthritis. Gold helps awaken a body's own healing energy. Blue clears the mind, and aqua is cooling and can ease fever.

3. *Topic Sentence:* _____

   _____

   To make a color wheel, draw a circle and divide it into twelve equal parts. Then color in each section, starting with red. Notice how you feel as you color each section. You may feel more drawn to some colors than to others. Some colors make you feel better than others. Think about which colors are good for your health.

CHAPTER TWO

And the Lucky Number Is . . .

→ four leaf clover

walk under a ladder is not luck
break mirror 7 years bad luck

Pre-Reading Activity

Discuss these questions.

1. What are the superstitions connected with the symbols in the pictures?
2. How superstitious are you?
3. What do you think is your lucky number?

Predicting

Answer the questions. Then compare your ideas with those in the reading.

1. Do any of these numbers have a special meaning in your culture?

   three four seven thirteen

2. What other cultures do you know of that give a special meaning to certain numbers?

And the Lucky Number Is . . .

[handwritten annotations: "thesis statement in at the end", "superstitions", "introduction", "topic", "control idea", "J. Century 13"]

Do you believe that seven is a lucky number or that things happen in sets of three? If so, your ideas are as old as Pythagoras, a Greek philosopher who lived 2,600 years ago. Pythagoras believed that certain numbers and their multiples had mystical power. For centuries, people have given importance to numbers and developed superstitions about them. Many of these superstitions have been passed on through the generations and still exist today.

Many of the superstitions surrounding numbers have a basis in science and nature. For example, early astrologers believed that seven planets governed the universe and therefore the lives of human beings. A seventh child was thought to have special gifts. Human life was divided into seven ages. Every seventh year was believed to bring great change. If a person's date of birth could be divided by seven, that person's life would be lucky. For the ancient Babylonians, three was a lucky number because it symbolized birth, life, and death. Some people still believe that a dream repeated three times comes true.

Numbers don't have the same meaning in all cultures. Five is considered a most holy and lucky number in Egypt. But in Ghana, the Ashanti people consider five to be an unlucky number. To give someone five of anything is to wish the person evil. The ancient Greeks and Egyptians thought the number four was a perfect number symbolizing unity, **endurance,** and balance. However, the Chinese consider the number four to be unlucky because it sounds like the word for death.

The number that seems to be almost universally considered unlucky is 13. No other number has had such a bad reputation for so long. The ancient Romans regarded it as a symbol of death, destruction, and **misfortune.** One of the earliest written stories about the number 13 appears in Norwegian mythology. This story tells about a feast at Valhalla to which 12 gods were invited. Loki, the god of evil, came uninvited, raising the number to 13. In the struggle to throw out Loki, Balder, the favorite of the gods, was killed.

There are many superstitions regarding the number 13. For example, in Britain it's considered a bad **omen** for 13 people to sit at a table. Some say that the person who rises first will meet with misfortune, even death, within a year. Others say it's the last person to rise. Some British people think it's unlucky to have 13 people in a room, especially for the person closest to the door. The thirteenth day of the month isn't considered a good day on which to begin any new **enterprise,** including marriage, or to set out on a journey. Many people believe that Friday the thirteenth is the unluckiest day in the year. This belief is so widespread that there are horror movies called *Friday the Thirteenth.*

Some people will go to great lengths to avoid the number 13. Hotel owners do not usually **assign** the number 13 to a room, preferring to label it 12A or 14 instead. The French never issue the house address 13, while in Italy the number 13 is **omitted** from the national lottery. Airlines have no thirteenth row on their planes, and office and apartment buildings rarely have a thirteenth floor.

From ancient civilizations to modern societies, the belief in the magic of numbers has **persisted** in spite of the advances in science and technology. There is nothing quite as stubborn as superstition. Even today in the twenty-first century, people still believe in bad luck and omens. In the future, people may work in space stations or travel the universe in starships, but there probably won't be a "Starbase 13" or a rocket liftoff on Friday the thirteenth. A seventh voyage will be a good one, and the third time around will still be lucky.

Vocabulary

Meaning

What are the meanings of the underlined words? Circle the letter of each correct answer.

1. Four was considered to be a perfect number symbolizing unity, <u>endurance</u>, and balance.
   a. persistence   c. independence
   continuing
   b. equality   (d.) strength

2. The Romans regarded 13 as a symbol of death, destruction, and <u>misfortune</u>.
   (a.) bad luck   c. injury
   b. opportunity   d. unhappiness

3. It's considered a bad <u>omen</u> for 13 people to sit at a table.
   a. promise   c. action
   (b.) sign   d. event

4. The thirteenth is not considered a good day on which to begin any new <u>enterprise</u>.
   a. building   c. journey
   (b.) project   d. meeting

5. Hotel owners will not usually <u>assign</u> the number 13 to a room.
   (a.) transfer   c. allow
   b. choose   (d.) give

6. In Italy, the number 13 is <u>omitted</u> from the lottery.
   (a.) left out   c. added
   b. repeated   d. replaced

7. The belief in the magic of numbers has <u>persisted</u>.
   a. gone away   c. changed
   b. become greater   (d.) continued

Word Building

Complete the sentences with the correct form of the word in capital letters. You may use your dictionary.

1. SUPERSTITION
    a. If you believe a broken mirror will bring misfortune, you are _superstitous_
    b. There are many _superstitions_ about the number 13.

2. LUCK
    a. Five is a _lucky_ number in Egypt.
    b. The ancient Babylonians believed that the number 3 would bring good _luck_.

3. BELIEVE
    a. Despite advances in science, many people still _Believe_ in the magic of numbers.
    b. There is a stubborn _beliefs_ that the number 13 will bring misfortune.

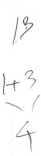

Comprehension

Looking for the Main Ideas

Circle the letter of the correct answer.

1. Throughout the ages, people have ___a___ .
   a. written stories about numbers
   b. given meaning and importance to numbers
   c. considered five a lucky number
   d. used numbers to tell the future

2. Numbers ___a___ .
   a. have different meanings in different cultures
   b. have the same meaning everywhere
   c. didn't have much meaning in ancient times
   d. don't have much meaning now

3. The number 13 ___d___ .
   a. is omitted from the lottery in every country
   b. was a good number for the ancient Romans
   c. is considered lucky in some countries
   d. is considered unlucky almost everywhere

Looking for Details

Scan the reading quickly to find the answers to these questions. Write complete sentences.

1. What was special about a seventh child?

   _____

   _____

2. What do some interpreters of dreams believe about a dream repeated three times?

   _____

   _____

3. What year was believed to bring change in a person's life?

   _____

   _____

4. Why was three a lucky number to the ancient Babylonians?

   _____

   _____

5. Where is five considered a holy and lucky number?

   _____

   _____

6. What did the number four symbolize to the ancient Greeks?

   _____

   _____

7. Where did one of the earliest written stories about the number 13 appear?

   _____

   _____

8. For what is the thirteenth day of the month considered unlucky?

   _____

   _____

9. What do hotel owners do to avoid assigning the number 13 to a room?

   _____

   _____

Making Inferences and Drawing Conclusions

The answers to these questions are not directly stated in the reading. Write complete sentences.

1. What influence did Pythagoras have on the beliefs we have about numbers?

   _____

   _____

2. Why might a seventh child be thought of as special?

   _____

   _____

3. Why would a hotel owner avoid assigning the number 13 to a room?

   _____

   _____

4. What effect have science and technology had on our belief in the power of numbers?

   _____

   _____

5. Why do people still believe in superstitions?

   _____

   _____

Discussion

Discuss these questions with your classmates.

1. What superstitions do you have in your country?
2. What are the lucky and unlucky numbers in your country?
3. Describe an object that is a symbol. Where and how is it used?

Organizing

Writing an Essay

An *essay* is a piece of writing that is several paragraphs long. An essay, just like a paragraph, is about one topic. Since its topic is broad, the essay is divided into paragraphs, one for each major point. To tie all the parts together, an introduction is added to the beginning and a conclusion to the end.

An essay has three parts:

1.   An introduction
2.   A body (one or more paragraphs)
3.   A conclusion

The *introduction* has two parts: general statements and a thesis statement. The *general statements* give the reader background information about the topic of the essay. These statements should get the reader interested in the topic. The *thesis statement* introduces the main idea of the essay. It is just like a topic sentence in a paragraph. It states the main topic and tells what will be said in the body paragraphs. The thesis is usually the last sentence of the introduction.

The *body* of the essay consists of one or more paragraphs. Each of these paragraphs has a topic sentence, supporting sentences, and sometimes a concluding sentence. The body paragraphs support whatever is stated in the thesis statement. The body paragraphs are similar to the supporting sentences of a paragraph.

The *conclusion* is the last paragraph of the essay. It summarizes the main points discussed in the body or restates the thesis in different words. It also leaves the reader with a final comment or thought about the topic.

Transitions or *linking words* are used to connect the paragraphs. These are just like the transitions used in paragraphs to connect ideas between sentences.

Look at the following diagram of an essay. Note how the parts of an essay correspond to the parts of a paragraph.

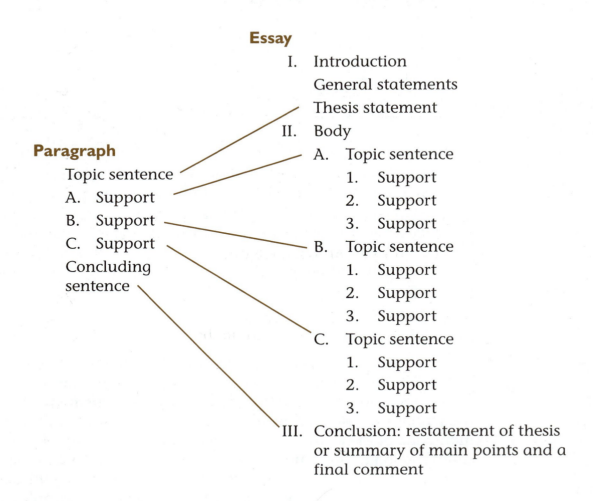

Essay

I.   Introduction
     General statements
     Thesis statement

II. Body
     A.   Topic sentence
          1.   Support
          2.   Support
          3.   Support
     B.   Topic sentence
          1.   Support
          2.   Support
          3.   Support
     C.   Topic sentence
          1.   Support
          2.   Support
          3.   Support

III. Conclusion: restatement of thesis
     or summary of main points and a
     final comment

Paragraph

Topic sentence
A.   Support
B.   Support
C.   Support
Concluding
sentence

The Thesis Statement

An essay is controlled by one main idea. This main idea is called the *thesis statement.* The thesis statement is similar to the topic sentence in a paragraph, but it is broader and gives the controlling idea for the whole essay. The topic sentence in each of the body paragraphs of an essay should relate to the thesis statement.

It is important to remember these points about a thesis statement.

1. The thesis statement should be a complete sentence.

2. The thesis statement should express an opinion, an idea, or a belief. The thesis statement should be something that you can argue about. It should not be a plain fact.

Example:

Not a thesis statement:
Water consists of hydrogen and oxygen.

Thesis statement:
The water in our homes may contain harmful chemicals.

3. The thesis statement should not be a detail or an example.

Example:

Not a thesis statement:
In Hong Kong, the number eight is lucky.

Thesis statement:
There are many superstitions about even numbers around the world.

4. The thesis statement may state or list how it will support an opinion.

Example:

Thesis statement:
Television has a bad influence on children for three main reasons.

Thesis statement:
The choice of food we eat during our New Year's festival in India is influenced by tradition and religion.

Thesis statments can not be a question

Read the following sentences. Some are thesis statements, and some are details. Put check marks next to the thesis statements.

✓ 1. People have always been superstitious about cats.

✗ 2. In certain parts of Asia, people believed that they became cats when they died.

✗ 3. It was thought that to cut your nails on Sunday would bring you bad luck.

✓ 4. There are many superstitions that are similar in several countries around the world.

✗ 5. There is a superstition among sailors that says wearing earrings will save a sailor from drowning.

✓ 6. It is believed that our health and physical condition have an effect on our dreams.

✗ 7. It is said that to knock over the salt on a table is to meet trouble.

✓ 8. Throughout history, the luck of odd numbers has been a matter of superstitious belief.

✗ 9. Dreams of fields, the sea, the country, and difficult roads and journeys are believed to be signs of heart trouble.

✓ 10. Many superstitions can be traced to ancient civilizations.

Read the following essay written by a student.

Model Essay

Superstitions in My Country

In the Middle East, especially Syria where I come from, people believe in some superstitions. Some of these superstitions are so strong that they are almost customs. These superstitions are about protecting against evil and bringing good luck. Two of the most popular superstitions are concerned with the evil eye and throwing water.

People believe that they must protect themselves from the evil eye of another person by putting turquoise beads in various places. A blue bead is pinned on newly born babies because babies are more vulnerable to an evil spirit and must be protected. Since houses must be protected, too, a blue bead, usually with a horseshoe, is placed near the doorway for protection against someone with an evil eye. Also, if people have an item of special value like a car or sewing machine, they must protect it with a blue bead.

Another popular superstition is throwing water, which is done at various times. When someone leaves on a trip, people throw water out of the window to wish the traveler a good trip. This is so the person will go and come back like water. Water is also thrown out when a funeral procession goes by the street, so that death will not come into their homes. The Armenians, who are Christians who live in Syria, throw water on each other on a special Saint's Day in mid-July for fertility and prosperity.

In conclusion, certain superstitions have become rituals with the purpose of protecting and bringing good luck. Because people always want to be protected and have good luck, these age-old superstitions are as strong today as they were ages ago and probably will continue in the future.

handwritten annotations: topic; controling idea is How; Controling idea is when; it is summerized T.S; T.S Thesis; Controling idea; T.S topic; final thought; 2 body pargraf; 4 pargra'

Look at the student essay on the previous page and complete the
following essay outline.

Essay Outline

I. Introduction

Thesis statement: _Two of the most_ _____

_____

II. Body

A. Topic sentence: _people belive that_ _____

_____

  1. Support: _babyis,_ _____

  _____

  2. Support: _houses_ _____

  _____

  3. Support: _Cars swing machin_ _____

  _____

B. Topic sentence: _Another popula_ _____

_____

  1. Support: _go to trip_ _____

  _____

  2. Support: _funeral pr— dean_ _____

  _____

  3. Support: _kristian_ _____

  _____

III. Conclusion

Do you know these symbols?

Circle the letter of the best answer.

1. When the bride and bridegroom leave the church in Western countries, rice or confetti (bits of paper) is showered on them. Why is confetti used?

    a. because paper is a symbol of life

    b. because confetti is less dangerous to the face and eyes than rice

    c. because rice is not found everywhere

2. What Japanese animal (worn as an amulet) is the symbol of abundance and riches?

    a. the fish   b. the eagle   c. the rabbit

3. In Burma, these animals are worn (as amulets) by children to protect them against the evil eye. In Italy, Greece, and Turkey, amber carvings of these animals are symbols of good health. What are these animals?

    a. dolphins   b. eagles   c. frogs

4. The wedding ring, a gold band that symbolizes never-ending love, is placed on the third finger of the left hand. Why is it placed on the third finger of the left hand?

    a. because that finger has no other use

    b. because it is believed that a nerve in that finger connects to the heart

    c. because that finger is a symbol of good health

5. The horseshoe is an ancient symbol of luck in the West. How is a horseshoe placed on the wall?

    a. It is placed with the ends pointing horizontally.

    b. It is placed with the ends pointing up.

    c. It is placed with the ends pointing down.

6. In the West, what does a ringing in one's right ear mean?

    a. It means you will get good news.

    b. It means you will get bad news.

    c. It means someone is saying bad things about you.

7. What color symbolizes love in Jewish traditions and symbolizes the south for the Navajo Indians?

a. red   b. blue   c. white

Video Activity • Changing Colors

1. The video shows colors that are *photochromic*—that change when light shines on them. Can you think of how this feature could be useful? Make a list of different possible uses.

2. Listen for the answers to these questions as you watch the video. Put a check mark before the correct answer.

   a. The flower on the young woman's T-shirt changes color when it is exposed to heat.

   _____ True _____ False

   b. The car turns from white to blue when sunlight is blocked.

   _____ True _____ False

   c. Which use for photochromic colors is *not* mentioned in the video?

   _____ toys   _____ food   _____ clothes
   _____ plastics   _____ money

   d. The main idea of the video is that

   _____ photochromic colors change in ultraviolet light.
   _____ TCS Industries makes 16 photochromic colors.
   _____ photochromic colors have many uses.

3. Discuss these questions:

   a. Would people enjoy wearing clothes that change colors in the light? Why or why not?

   b. Could these colors be used in homes or other buildings to change people's attitudes? Could they help heal people? If so, how?

Internet Activity

- Look up "numerology" on the Internet. What interesting facts can you find? What do the numbers of your birth date mean? Tell your class.

- What was your opinion of the sites you visited? Did you believe the information they contained? Why or why not?

Customs

CHAPTER THREE

An American Holiday, Hawaiian Style

Pre-Reading Activity

Discuss these questions.

1. What is happening in the picture?
2. What do you know about Hawaii?
3. How do you think Hawaiians might celebrate Thanksgiving?

Predicting

Can you guess the meanings of these Hawaiian words? Write down your guesses. Then compare your answers with those in the reading.

1. Hawaiians celebrate July Fourth with a big *luau* for all their friends and family. party
2. They often wear colorful *muumuus* at celebrations. clothing
3. Around their necks they wear *leis* made from flowers.
4. The pig is roasted in an *imu*. dish

An American Holiday, Hawaiian Style

Fireworks. Hot dogs. Bands marching down Main Street. These are the pictures that come to many people's minds when they think of U.S. holidays. But the United States is a vast country made up of people from many different cultures, and the celebration of holidays reflects this diversity.

In the Chinatown section of San Francisco, rice and snow peas are a part of many holiday meals. In New Mexico, one might encounter chili peppers, *piñatas,* and Mexican music on the Fourth of July. In Hawaii, one popular way to celebrate a holiday is with a feast, or *luau,* which has been a Hawaiian tradition for centuries.

[handwritten: food]

Hawaii is the only state in the United States that was once an independent country with its own language and culture. Today, many Hawaiians continue to celebrate traditional Hawaiian holidays, such as Prince Kuhio Day, Kamehameha Day, and Aloha Week. In celebration of their Hawaiian ancestry, Islanders might dress in traditional clothes such as loose dresses called *muumuus* or colorful shirts. Around their necks they might wear *leis,* or rings of flowers.

Even when it comes to celebrating a traditional American holiday such as Thanksgiving, Hawaiians give it their own special flavor. They might place pumpkins on doorsteps and **paste** cardboard pilgrims on windows, but chances are there will also be a turkey or a pig roasting under the ground in an earth oven, or *imu.*

Cooking in an *imu* is an ancient Islands custom that requires much work and cooperation among family members. Preparations begin several days before Thanksgiving, when the family goes down to the beach or to the mouth of a stream to fill sacks with smooth, rounded lava stones. They choose the stones carefully for their shape and size and for the presence of holes that will prevent the rocks from exploding when they are heated.

[handwritten: earth oven]

To prepare the *imu,* the men first dig a large hole in the shape of a bowl about three feet wide and two feet deep. They then **line** the bottom and sides of the hole with the lava rocks. Firewood is cut and **piled up,** ready for the holiday morning when a fire is lit inside the hole. As the fire gets bigger and hotter, more rocks are placed in the hole. Finally, the lava rocks get so hot that they glow red and white. The fire is then brushed aside, and several of the hot rocks are placed inside the turkey or pig. The meat is then wrapped in the long, broad leaves of the *ti* plant and tied up tightly with wire.

Before the pig or turkey is placed in the *imu,* chopped pieces of banana plant are spread over the hot rocks. The white, juicy lining of this plant makes a lot of steam, but it can also cause a bitter taste, so *ti* leaves are layered over it. Finally, the pig or turkey is placed in the *imu,* along with sweet potatoes, pineapple, plantain, vegetables, and even fresh fish—all wrapped in *ti* leaves.

More hot rocks are spread over the **bundles** of food, then more *ti* leaves, a layer of wet sacks, and a canvas covering. Dirt is **shoveled** into the hole and **patted down** smoothly. Not a **trace** can be seen of either the meal or the earth oven in which it is cooking.

Three to four hours later, the dirt is shoveled away. The men dip their hands in cold water and then quickly remove the burned leaves and rocks, allowing delicious smells to **emerge** from the oven. The bundles of cooked food are taken out, uncovered, and placed on platters, ready for a different kind of Thanksgiving meal, cooked and served Hawaiian style.

Vocabulary

Meaning

Complete each definition with one of the following words.

line	piled up	patted down
trace	emerge	pasted
bundles	shovel	

1. A number of things one on top of the other are ~~atop~~ *piled up*.

2. Something stuck to something else with paste is *pasted* to it.

3. A *trace* is a sign that something existed in a certain place.

4. If you wanted something to be *patted down*, you would tap or hit it gently to flatten or smooth it.

5. To cover the inside of something is to ~~piled up~~ ^shovel^ it. ^like^ ^line the ~~door~~ through^

6. To __emerge__ is to come into view.

7. When digging a hole in the ground, if you lift and throw the dirt with a special tool, you __~~have~~ shovel__. ^don't shovel your lot^

8. __bundles__ are groups of things fastened or tied together.

Word Building

Complete the sentences with the correct form of the word in capital letters. You may use your dictionary.

1. CELEBRATE
   a. Hawaiians like to _____ special holidays with a big feast.
   b. The _____ of July Fourth differs according to where you are in the United States.

2. TRADITION
   a. _____ Hawaiian clothes have flowers on them.
   b. It is a Hawaiian _____ to wear necklaces of flowers.

3. CARE
   a. Hawaiians choose the stones for the imu _____.
   b. The men have to be very _____ when removing the burned leaves and rocks.

Comprehension

Looking for the Main Ideas

Circle the letter of the correct answer.

1. American holidays _____.
   a. are not usually celebrated by Hawaiians
   b. are not celebrated in the same way throughout the United States
   c. are similar to ancient Islands customs
   d. are not celebrated everywhere in the United States

2. Hawaiians celebrate Thanksgiving _____.
   a. at a different time of year than other Americans
   b. in the same way that they celebrate all their holidays
   c. with some typically American and some Hawaiian customs
   d. because it is an old Hawaiian tradition

3. The steps that are taken to prepare a Hawaiian Thanksgiving dinner _____.
   a. are done by one individual in each community
   b. involve the women only
   c. have little to do with native Hawaiian traditions
   d. begin several days in advance of the holiday

Looking for Details

Complete the following sentences.

1. A popular way to celebrate a holiday in Hawaii is with a _____.

2. The Hawaiians like to roast their pig or turkey in _____.

3. Before Thanksgiving, family members go down to the beach to _____.

4. After the men dig a large hole, they _____.

5. When the lava rocks are so hot that they glow, then _____.

6. Three items that are placed in the oven with the pig or turkey are _____, _____, and _____.

7. After the hot rocks are spread over the food, _____, _____, and _____ are placed over the rocks.

8. _____ hours after the oven is covered, the dirt is shoveled away.

Making Inferences and Drawing Conclusions

The answers to these questions are not directly stated in the reading. Write complete sentences.

1. Why are American holidays celebrated differently in certain parts of the United States?

   _____

   _____

2. How is Hawaii different from the other states in the United States?

   _____

   _____

3. Why do Islanders dress in traditional clothes on holidays?

   _____

   _____

4. How are preparations for a Hawaiian Thanksgiving a family affair?

   _____

   _____

5. Why is dirt shoveled over the hole for the *imu* and patted down?

   _____

   _____

Discussion

Discuss these questions with your classmates.

1. Describe a method of barbecuing in your country.

2. Describe a very old tradition that is still practiced during your holidays and festivals.

3. Are there certain tasks that men do and women do during a preparation for a special festival or occasion?

Read the following essay written by a student. Underline the thesis statement and the topic sentence in each of the body paragraphs.

Model Essay

The Dragon Boat Festival

The Dragon Boat Festival is a significant festival in Chinese traditional celebrations. The Dragon Boat Festival is celebrated on the fifth day of lunar May. This holiday is to commemorate the death of Chyu Yuan, a well-loved poet of the fourth century B.C. Chyu Yuan drowned himself to protest his king's despotic rule. The villagers respected him so much that they rowed their boats down the river and dropped chung-tze, rice dumplings, into the river to feed the fish, so the fish would not eat Chyu Yuan's body. To celebrate the Dragon boat Festival, families do several things, like make chung-tze, hang the moxa herb, and watch the dragon boat race.

Before the Dragon Boat Festival, every family prepares chung-tze. This is a kind of rice dumpling filled with various things, such as bean curd, meat, mushrooms, and shrimp, and then wrapped in bamboo leaves and steamed. The mother and the children all work together in preparing the chung-tze.

Then each family also has to buy moxa herb and hang it in a special location. The reason for this is that the moxa herb can get rid of the bad luck in the family atmosphere. Some people even use these herbs to wash sick babies, for they believe that this special festival can bring some "transformation" in people's lives. Usually the father and the boys find a location to hang the moxa herb.

After preparing the chung-tze, each family goes to the river to watch the dragon boat race, which takes place on this festival. The dragon boat race symbolizes the story of Chyu Yuan. It is a rowing boat team competition with about thirty people on each team. All the spectators cheer and shout enthusiastically. After the exciting race, both the competitors and the spectators usually eat many chung-tze.

The Dragon Boat Festival symbolizes the unique meanings of Chinese history; furthermore, the process of making the rice dumplings, the hanging of the moxa herb, and the boat race are a way of drawing all members of the family together again. Perhaps one day we will have a very different celebration, but so far I still like this holiday being celebrated in a traditional way.

Organizing

Chronological Order

Chronological order means time order. In writing an essay, time order is often used to describe events over a period of time in a person's life or during a historical event. Time order can also be used to show how something works or the steps in a process.

In all kinds of chronological order or time order essays, you should use transition signals and time expressions to make the time sequence clear. The following are some time order words and phrases:

First, . . . (Second, third, etc.)
Next, . . . The next step, . . .
Then . . .
Finally, . . . Last, . . .
Before . . . / After . . .
Meanwhile,
Three hours later, . . .
In the morning, . . .
At 6 o'clock,

Look back at the reading and underline the words that show time order in the preparation of the Hawaiian Thanksgiving dinner.

The Introduction

The *introduction* of an essay
has two parts:

1. General statements *to specific statement*
2. A thesis statement

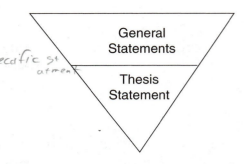

General
Statements

Thesis
Statement

The first statement in an introduction should be a *general statement* about the topic. The second sentence should be less general, the third sentence should be even less general, and so on until the reader comes to the thesis statement. The number of general statements you write in an introduction depends on how long your essay is. However, you should write at least two or three general statements in an introduction.

General Statements

• Introduce the topic of the essay
• Give background information on the topic

The *thesis statement* is often the last sentence of the introduction. It is the most important sentence in the introduction. It gives the specific topic and the controlling ideas for the whole essay. It may list the subtopics that will be discussed in the body paragraphs and may state the method of organization.

The Thesis Statement

• Is often the last sentence of the introduction
• States the specific topic
• May state the subtopics
• May state the method of organization

Exercise 1

On the next page are introductory paragraphs for essays describing a series of events on a special day. The sentences in these introductions are not in the correct order. Rewrite each introduction, beginning with the most general statement and ending with the thesis.

Introduction 1:

(1) Sometimes weddings are planned more than a year in advance because there are many events and procedures that must not be forgotten. (2) The traditional American wedding is formal and has many steps, each of which has a symbolic meaning. (3) Most people love their wedding day and remember it for the rest of their lives. (4) A great deal of preparation and expense go into planning a wedding.

Introduction 2:

(1) April Fool's Day is celebrated on the first of April in most countries. (2) If, like me, you don't know what day it is, you may be in for a surprise. (3) It is a day when people have a lot of fun. (4) People often play tricks on each other. (5) Last April Fool's Day is a day I will never forget because three very surprising things happened to me.

Introduction 3:

(1) The reason for the festivities is explained in stories handed down through generations. (2) Ga Homowo is a festival of Thanksgiving celebrated by the Ga people of Ghana. (3) They had the first festival after the harvest, and it is now celebrated annually. (4) Unlike most annual festivals, Ga Homowo is made up of a series of events and celebrated within family groups. (5) These stories trace the origin of Ga Homowo to the first immigrants of the Ga tribe who landed on the shores of Ghana.

Introduction 4:

(1) It was on this day in 1776 that the original 13 colonies declared their independence from England. (2) There is a series of events in which people can participate. (3) Americans celebrate their day of independence on the Fourth of July. (4) A new nation was born. (5) In celebration of that day, people get together with friends and family.

Writing Practice

Choose an important occasion in your country. Write an introduction for an essay on how you prepare for this occasion. Include general statements and a thesis.

CHAPTER FOUR

Hop to It!

Pre-Reading Activity

Discuss these questions.
1. What is happening in the picture?
2. What other events with animals do you know about?
3. What do you think of training animals for performance?

Predicting

Which of the following words do you think relate to frogs? Circle them and say how you think they are connected to the topic. Then compare your ideas with those in the reading.

jump	jockey	scream
race	whistle	launching pad

"He's good enough for one thing, I should judge—he can outjump any frog in Calaveras County," said Smiley in Mark Twain's famous short story "The Celebrated Jumping Frog of Calaveras County." This was the **inspiration** for the Calaveras County Jumping Frog Contest, which has taken place since 1928 in the village of Angels Camp in Calaveras County, California. The first year, 15,000 people attended this unusual event, more than the entire population of Calaveras County at the time. The following year, the crowd doubled, and by 1931, the event was so popular that two additional jumping areas had to be added to **accommodate** entries from around the world. Today, more than 50,000 spectators attend this event and the frog entries number 1,000.

Although the Calaveras County Jumping Frog Contest has gained international attention, the majority of the competitors are still people from Calaveras County. Anyone who would like to enter goes to the registration table, fills out a form, and pays a **modest** entry fee. The fee includes the cost of renting a frog in case the entrant doesn't already own one. Many people who live in the area go out and catch their frogs the night before, so they are "fresh" and ready to go on the day of the contest.

After entering the contest, the competitors must decide who will be the "jockey." This is the person who places the frog on the **launching pad** and then encourages the frog to jump. The goals of the entrants and their "jockeys" are, first of all, to have fun; second, to win a prize; and third, to set a new world frog-jumping record.

The contest starts when the "jockey" positions his or her frog and then yells, screams, jumps up and down, puffs, blows, whistles, or does whatever else is necessary to **incite** the frog to jump. The one thing that is not allowed is any kind of physical contact with the frog. Each frog is given 15 seconds to jump three times. Once a frog has made its three jumps, an official measures the distance from the center of the pad to the spot where the frog landed on its third jump. Naturally, the winning frog is usually the one that jumped in the straightest line rather than zigzagged around. Some frogs **frustrate** their "jockeys" by jumping back toward the launching pad after a spectacular first or second jump.

Like any of nature's creations, frogs are **unpredictable**—that is, unless they have been to Bill Steed's famous Croaker College. Steed's "students" are given a 240-hour frog training course to teach them the **fundamentals** of frog jumping under pressure. At Croaker College, the frogs work out in a pool, lift tiny weights, do chin-ups and high dives, eat centipede soup and ladybug salad, and generally prepare for the big day. Do graduates of Croaker College really win frog-jumping contests more often? That's a question Jim Steed prefers not to answer.

After the winners have been announced and the prizes given, the participants can take their frogs (or return their "rentals") and go home, or they can stay and enjoy the rest of the Calaveras County Fair. They can listen to country music, view craft displays, attend a horse race, watch a farm animal **auction**, and more. For those people who think nothing quite compares to the excitement of the jumping frogs, however, there is the **consolation** of knowing there is always next year.

Vocabulary

Meaning

What are the meanings of the underlined words? Circle the letter of the correct answer.

1. This is the <u>inspiration</u> for the Calaveras County Jumping Frog Contest.
   - a. influence
   - b. information
   - c. description
   - d. advertisement

2. Two jumping areas had to be added to <u>accommodate</u> the entries from around the world.
   - a. invite
   - b. announce
   - c. encourage
   - d. provide for

3. Anyone who would like to enter pays a <u>modest</u> entry fee.
   - a. small
   - b. expensive
   - c. formal
   - d. official

4. The "jockey" places the frog on the <u>launching pad</u>.
   a. winner's circle   c. measuring place
   b. take-off point   d. finish line

5. The "jockey" does whatever is necessary to <u>incite</u> the frog to jump.
   a. excite   c. demonstrate
   b. calm   d. frighten

6. Some frogs <u>frustrate</u> their "jockeys."
   a. upset   c. stop
   b. satisfy   d. reward

7. Frogs are <u>unpredictable</u>.
   a. experienced   c. native
   b. surprising   d. understandable

8. At Croaker College, frogs are taught the <u>fundamentals</u> of jumping.
   a. possibilities   c. origins
   b. basics   d. tricks

9. People can attend a farm animal <u>auction</u> at the fair.
   a. show   c. race
   b. contest   d. sale

10. There is the <u>consolation</u> of knowing there's always next year.
    a. pressure   c. excitement
    b. benefit   d. comfort

Word Building

Complete the sentences with the correct form of the word in capital letters. You may use your dictionary.

1. COMPETITION
    a. The _____ try to make the frogs jump as far as possible.
    b. The contest can get very _____ when people start to yell and scream at their frogs.

2. ENTER
   a. You must pay an _____ fee if you want to take part in the competition.
   b. The _____ are not allowed to touch their frogs during the contest.

3. PREDICT
   a. It is not easy to _____ which way a frog will jump.
   b. Frogs do not always jump in a _____ direction.

Comprehension

Looking for the Main Ideas

Circle the letter of the correct answer.

1. The Calaveras County Jumping Frog Contest _____.
   a. is an expensive but popular event
   b. is a formal international event
   c. is an unusual but popular event
   d. is not a popular event

2. The Jumping Frog Contest _____.
   a. is open to everyone, even those without frogs
   b. is open only to graduates of Croaker College
   c. is open only to people with frogs caught in the area
   d. is open only to people from Calaveras County

3. The purpose of the contest is _____.
   a. to find the best frogs in the world
   b. to advertise Calaveras County frogs
   c. for people to learn about frogs
   d. for people to have a good time

Looking for Details

Scan the reading quickly to find the answers to these questions. Write complete sentences.

1. Where did the idea for the Jumping Frog Contest come from?

   _____

   _____

2. How often does the Jumping Frog Contest take place?

   _____

   _____

3. Approximately how many people attend the Jumping Frog Contest today?

   _____

   _____

4. What does the entry fee include?

   _____

   _____

5. What can people do if they don't have a frog?

   _____

   _____

6. What does the "jockey" do?

   _____

   _____

7. How many jumps must the frog make before an official measures the distance?

   _____

   _____

8. List three things Bill Steed's students do in their training course.

   _____

   _____

Making Inferences and Drawing Conclusions

The answers to these questions are not directly stated in the reading. Write complete sentences.

1. Why is the Calaveras County Jumping Frog Contest so popular?

   _____

   _____

2. Why do you think there is only a modest entry fee?

   _____

   _____

3. Why would a "jockey" be frustrated if his or her frog jumped back to the launching pad?

   _____

   _____

4. Why are frogs unpredictable?

   _____

   _____

5. How do the competitors feel during this contest?

   _____

   _____

Discussion

Discuss these questions with your classmates.

1. What special event that is not a holiday takes place in your country every year?

2. What customs in the United States or in other countries seem unusual to you?

3. Describe an event that requires special clothing or costumes.

Organizing

The Conclusion

The final paragraph of your essay is the *conclusion.* It tells the reader you have completed your essay. In the conclusion, you either summarize the main points in the body of your essay or rewrite the thesis statement using different words. Then you add a final comment or thought on the subject.

Begin your conclusion with a transition signal such as

In conclusion, . . .

In summary, . . .

To summarize, . . .

The Conclusion

* Summarizes the main points or restates the thesis in different words and

* Includes a final comment or thought on the subject

Exercise 1

Write conclusions for essays with the following introductions. The first one is done for you.

Introduction 1:

On October 31, Americans celebrate Halloween. Halloween means "holy evening." This is the evening before the Christian holy day of All Saints Day. However, Halloween is older than Christianity. Before Christianity, people in Britain believed that the ghosts of the dead came back on this day, and so they had rituals to scare the ghosts. Immigrants came from Europe to America and brought with them the custom of Halloween, as well as the many symbols and activities associated with this day.

Conclusion 1:

In conclusion, Halloween as it is celebrated in the United States today still has many of the symbols and rituals brought over by the European immigrants. Although it is an old custom, it is a lot of fun. People will continue to celebrate Halloween for a long time to come.

Introduction 2:

Like other countries, Japan has its own strict rules for table manners. These rules date back to the sixteenth century when the Ogasawara system of manners was developed. With the creation of this system, table manners reached an art form. These rules involve how the food is served, how the chopsticks are handled, and the order in which the foods are eaten.

Conclusion 2:

_____

_____

_____

_____

Introduction 3:

Birthday celebrations have been around for more than 5,000 years. In every part of the world, birthdays are celebrated in a slightly different way. One traditional American birthday celebration was brought over by the Europeans. The elements, such as a birthday song, a cake, candles, and gifts, are symbolic. In the United States, many birthday celebrations involve these elements.

Conclusion 3:

_____

_____

_____

_____

Writing Practice

Write an introduction and conclusion for an essay describing a local custom or event in your country.

Do you know these customs?

Circle T if the sentence is true. Circle F if the sentence is false.

1. In Scotland on New Year's Eve, most people eat haggis
   (stuffed sheep's intestine), turnips, and potatoes.   T   F
2. It is a custom for holy men and women in India to wear
   the color white.   T   F
3. In Turkey, whenever a person drinks Turkish coffee, he or
   she must turn the cup over on the saucer for good fortune.   T   F
4. In Mexico, it is the custom to shower the bride with paper
   money as she dances at the wedding reception.   T   F
5. In Hawaii and Oceania, the New Year festival, called
   makahki, is celebrated in mid-October.   T   F
6. The custom of decorating trees at Christmas started in
   England in the 1700s.   T   F

Video Activity • A New England Clambake   CNN

1. Clams are a kind of shellfish found in the ocean off the coast of
   New England. The video shows a clambake, which is a typical New
   England custom during the summer months. This custom may have
   come originally from a native American custom. Review these words
   before watching the video:

   quahog (pronounced *ko-hog*): a type of clam

   chowder: a thick seafood soup

   Nantucket: an island off the coast of Massachusetts

2. Which of the following foods are shown in the video?

   ____ onions   ____ clams   ____ tomatoes   ____ potatoes
   ____ beans   ____ lobster   ____ clam chowder ____ garlic

3. Number the following steps in the correct order, as shown in the video.

   ____ Add the clams.

   ____ Heat the rocks with a fire.

   ____ Dig a pit.

   ____ Set down rocks.

4. Write a brief description of a New England clambake based on the video. Do you know of any similar customs in other countries?

Internet Activity

- Use the Internet to find out about these celebrations and where they are held: Fasching, Mardi Gras, Obon, Inti Raymi, and Songkran.

- Write a short description of one celebration based on your research and tell the class about it. Which web sites provided the best information and who created them?

Mind and Body

CHAPTER FIVE

Bumps and Personalities

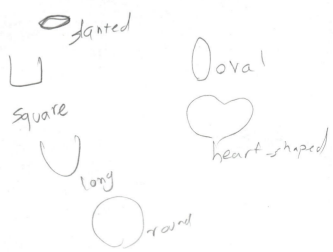

slanted

square

long

oval

heart-shaped

round

Pre-Reading Activity

Discuss these questions.

1. What do the eyes of the person in the picture tell you?
2. How does the shape of a person's face tell you about the person?
3. Do people have different shaped heads? What does a person's head shape tell you about the person?

Predicting

Which parts of the head and face do you associate with each of the following characteristics? Compare your ideas with those in the reading.

1. _a_ nose   a. curiosity
2. _e_ lips   b. self-confidence
3. _d_ eyes   c. decisiveness   having the power to decide
4. _b_ shape of face   d. creativity
5. _c_ eyebrows   e. pride

Bumps and Personalities

40

Have you ever been afraid of or attracted to someone just because of the way the person looks? When you first meet someone, it is not unusual to react to his or her appearance. But these are first impressions, and most people assume that it takes time to find out what someone is really like. It is possible, however, that a person's appearance **reveals** more than we realize. According to some experts, a person's face, head, and body can reveal a great deal about personality.

Since ancient times, people have practiced the art of physiognomy, or reading character from physical features. The ancient Greeks compared the human face to the faces of various animals and birds, such as the eagle and the horse. They believed people shared certain character **traits** with the animals they resembled. A person with an equine, or horselike, face was thought to be loyal, brave, and **stern.** A person with an aquiline, or eaglelike, nose was believed to be bold and courageous, as well as **arrogant** and self-centered.

Physiognomists study such features as the shape of the head, the length and thickness of the neck, the color and thickness of the hair, and the shape of the nose, mouth, eyes, and chin. They believe that round-faced people are self-confident. **Prominent** cheekbones show strength of character, while a pointed nose reveals curiosity. Heavy arched eyebrows belong to a decisive individual, while thin arched eyebrows signal a restless and active personality. Almond-shaped eyes reveal an artistic nature. Round, soft eyes belong to dreamers. Down-turned lips reveal a proud character, while a long, pointed chin **indicates** someone who likes to give orders.

A related—though not as ancient—art is phrenology, the study of the bumps on the head. Phrenologists have identified 40 bumps of various shapes and sizes on the human head. They "read" these bumps to identify a person's talents and character. For example, a bump between the nose and forehead is said to be present in people who have natural elegance and a love of beauty. A bump behind the curve of the ear is the sign of a courageous and adventurous person.

achieve

Phrenologists are not so much interested in health as they are in character and personality. They believe, for example, that a **bulge** in the center of the forehead is typical of people who have a good memory and a desire for knowledge. A small bump at the top of the head indicates a person who has strong moral character, while a bump just below this one is a sign of generosity and a kind, good nature. Phrenologists say a bump just above the tip of the eyebrow is found in people who love order and discipline, and a rise at the very back of the head is evident in people who are very attached to their families.

Phrenology was developed in the early eighteenth century by Franz Joseph Gall, a doctor in Vienna. His interest began at school when he noticed that boys with prominent eyes seemed to have the best memories. This led him to believe that a connection existed between appearance and ability. Dr. Gall's research interested many people, but he was **ridiculed** by other doctors. When he died in 1828, he was a poor and **bitter** man. It was only many years later that Dr. Gall's theories found support among some doctors and scientists, and today the art of phrenology has become more accepted.

Vocabulary

Meaning

What are the meanings of the underlined words? Circle the letter of each correct answer.

1. A person's face can <u>reveal</u> a great deal about personality. *show*
    a. show
    b. cover up
    c. hold
    d. identify

2. The ancient Greeks believed that people shared certain character <u>traits</u> with animals.
    a. features
    b. movements
    c. habits
    d. connections

3. A person with a horselike face might be proud and <u>stern</u>. *strikes*
    a. noble
    b. serious
    c. quiet
    d. confident

4. A person with an eaglelike nose was believed to be <u>arrogant</u> and self-centered.
   a. honest   c. lonely
   (b.) proud   d. brave

5. <u>Prominent</u> cheekbones show strength of character.
   a. healthy   (c.) noticeable
   b. hollow   d. flat

6. A long, pointed chin <u>indicates</u> someone who likes to give orders.
   a. covers up   c. encourages
   (b.) points out   d. describes

7. A <u>bulge</u> in the center of the forehead is typical of people with a good memory.
   (a.) lump   c. point
   b. hole   d. mark

8. Dr. Gall was <u>ridiculed</u> by other doctors.
   a. praised   c. ignored
   b. questioned   (d.) laughed at

9. He died a poor and <u>bitter</u> man.
   a. hopeful   c. faithful
   (b.) unhappy   d. popular

Word Building

Complete the sentences with the correct form of the word in capital letters. You may use your dictionary.

1. DECIDE
   a. A person who can choose quickly and doesn't change his or her mind is _decided (adj)_
   b. Arched eyebrows are said to indicate someone who can make ___decisions___

(swelling)

2. COURAGE
   a. A person who is brave is also _courageous_
   b. A bump behind your ear is said to be a sign of _courage_.

3. SCIENCE
   a. Many _scientist_ thought Dr. Gall's research was ridiculous.
   b. It was difficult to find _scinece_ proof for Dr. Gall's theories.

Comprehension

Looking for the Main Ideas

Circle the letter of the correct answer.

1. Physiognomists believe that _____.
   a. you can improve your personality by studying your face
   b. the head is the most important part of the body
   c. physical features reveal personality
   d. people are like animals in many ways

2. Phrenologists _____.
   a. "read" the bumps on people's heads to treat their health problems
   b. compare bumps on heads to see who is more attractive
   c. believe the eyes are the "mirror of the soul"
   d. study bumps on the head to determine character traits

3. Dr. Gall's ideas _____.
   a. were at first not accepted by other doctors
   b. were immediately considered the work of a genius
   c. are no longer discussed
   d. made him admired in his lifetime

Looking for Details

Circle T if the sentence is true. Circle F if the sentence is false.

1. Physiognomy is a modern practice.   T   (F)

2. The ancient Greeks compared the human face to
   those of animals.   (T)   F

3. Phrenologists have identified 25 bumps on the head.   T   (F)

4. A bump on the forehead is a sign of courage.   T   (F)

5. Physiognomists study the shape of the head, face,
   and body.   T   (F)

6. Physiognomists believe that round-faced people are
   self-confident.   (T)   F

7. Phrenology is a much more ancient art than
   physiognomy.   T   (F)

8. Dr. Gall's research did not interest many people.   (T)   F

9. Dr. Gall was rewarded for his research later in life.   (T)   F

Making Inferences and Drawing Conclusions

The answers to the questions are not directly stated in the reading.
Write complete answers.

1. Why did the Greeks compare humans to animals?

   _____

   _____

2. Why did Dr. Gall want to study phrenology?

   _____

   _____

3. Why did other doctors ridicule Dr. Gall's research?

   _____

   _____

4. Why did Dr. Gall die a poor and bitter man?

   _____

   _____

5. What might a physiognomist say about someone with a long nose, thin eyebrows, and almond-shaped eyes?

   _____

   _____

Discussion

Discuss these questions with your classmates.

1. What characteristics of the face and body show good health? What characteristics show bad health?

2. According to your astrological sign, what character traits are you supposed to have? Do you fit the description?

3. Do you think that astrology is more precise than physiognomy or phrenology?

4. Look at the diagram of the 40 possible bumps on the head and examine your own bumps. How well do your bumps correspond with your personality?

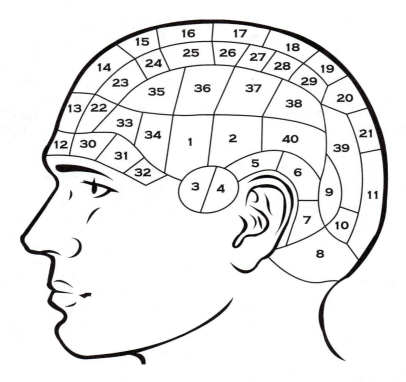

1. **The music bump**
   This bump is a sign of a natural talent for music and artistic creativity.
2. **The money bump**
   This bump shows the need to earn and save money.
3. **The mathematics bump**
   This bump, which is in the center of the temple, is a sign of a scientific and logical mind.
4. **The greed bump**
   This bump is found in people who are greedy about food and cannot control their appetites.
5. **The business bump**
   This bump is a sign of a practical person with a good sense of business. People with a bump here find it hard to relax.
6. **The courage bump**
   This bump is a sign of courage and adventure.
7. **The strength bump**
   This bump appears in a person who has physical or mental energy.
8. **The love bump**
   This bump appears in people who are passionate, jealous, or sensual.

9. **The fighting bump**
   This bump reveals a competitive character in a person. This person is usually very determined to achieve something.
10. **The affection bump**
    A bump here shows a person with an affectionate character who can love and show tenderness.
11. **The parental bump**
    A protrusion in this area reveals that a person has a strong motherly or fatherly instinct.
12. **The aesthetic bump**
    A bump here shows that a person has a strong love of beauty and elegance.
13. **The studying bump**
    This bump is found in people who love knowledge and have a good memory.
14. **The meditative bump**
    This bump appears in people who like to meditate and analyze.
15. **The justice bump**
    This bump reveals a person who has a strong sense of what is right and what is wrong.
16. **The kindness bump**
    A bump in this area is a sign of a person who is kind and generous.

17. *The bump of spirituality*
This bump on the top of the head shows that the person has a strong spiritual mind.

18. *The bump of willpower*
This bump shows willpower, determination, and reliability in a person.

19. *The bump of authority*
This bump is a sign of a person who likes to make decisions and control other people.

20. *The bump of concentration*
This bump belongs to a person with a strong ability to concentrate, particularly on intellectual matters.

21. *The family bump*
This bump appears in people who are attached to their families.

22. *The travel bump*
A bump in this area reveals someone who loves to travel and move from one place to another. This person will feel comfortable wherever he or she is.

23. *The logic bump*
This bump shows a logical person who has a strong sense of reasoning.

24. *The flexible mind bump*
A bump here shows that a person has an open and flexible mind.

25. *The bump of conformity*
This is the bump of someone who likes to conform to what is expected and obeys conventions, such as following the latest fashion.

26. *The bump of idealism*
This bump reveals a person who has strong ideals.

27. *The bump of optimism*
This bump shows that a person is optimistic about life and believes in other people.

28. *The bump of success*
A bump in this area indicates that a person puts all his or her efforts and energy into succeeding in life.

29. *The critical bump*
This bump shows that a person can look objectively at things and criticize himself or herself as well as others.

30. *The objectivity bump*
This bump is developed in people who can put themselves in someone else's place and understand the other person's situation.

31. *The color bump*
This bump shows that a person has a strong sense of color, as shown in either clothes or surroundings.

32. *The bump of meticulousness*
This bump indicates a meticulous, orderly, neat, and precise person.

33. *The organization bump*
This bump is found in people who organize their time very efficiently so that not a moment is lost.

34. *The rhythm bump*
This bump is developed in musicians and singers who have a strong sense of rhythm.

35. *The bump of gregariousness*
This bump is seen in people who like to be with others and are very outgoing, communicative, warm, and happy.

36. *The originality bump*
A bump in this area shows that a person has an original character and likes to be different and creative.

37. *The inventive bump*
This bump is a sign of a person who can create new things and be inventive.

38. *The bump of fame*
This bump shows that a person wants to be known and recognized by others. Many famous people have this bump.

39. *The bump of caution*
This bump belongs to a person who is very careful about everything.

40. *The bump of tactfulness*
This bump shows that a person is tactful, polite, and diplomatic with others.

Read the following essay written by a student. Underline the thesis statement and the topic sentence in each of the body paragraphs.

Model Essay

A Virgo

Every person has both good and bad character traits. Most people do not like to be criticized by others. It is good to be honest with yourself. We must admit that we all have both good and bad traits, and we must like ourselves as we are. If people do not love even a part of themselves, then they are practically dead. Since I am going to write about myself, I will write about the good and bad traits of my character. I was born under the sign Virgo, and I believe I have some of the characteristics of people born under this sign.

One example of a good trait of a Virgo that I have is patience. Sometimes I think I am almost too patient, but I have also found that patience helps me in a lot of things. For example, it helps me to study when the lesson is difficult or boring. Also, if I don't succeed in something, I am willing to try several more times. My patience also helps me to relax and stay calm. I am very patient with people, too, e.g., children, senior citizens, and even people who are sick and need a lot of help. I can deal with people who are nervous, angry, and upset and help them to calm down. Sometimes people take advantage of my patience, however, and I don't like that at all.

Another example of a trait that I have, which is typical of a Virgo, is ambition. I am very ambitious and can't sit in one place for more than ten minutes. If I make up my mind to do something, then I will do anything to meet my goal, no matter how long it takes and how much energy and time will be needed to accomplish it. This is what helped me to graduate from high school in three years. I like to do housework, cook, and take care of babies. I also like to work outside my home. I like to be busy all day and have lots of things to do. This makes me happy and satisfied. I hate sitting at home all day doing nothing.

Finally, like anyone, Virgos have some bad traits, too. This ambition can sometimes make them take on more work than they can handle, leading them to strain themselves to a breaking point. Sometimes I take on too much work and then reach a point at which I can do no more. Then I have to rest for a while and regain my strength. Virgos can also be fussy and irritable. I suppose I can be that way too sometimes. For instance, I like everything to be neat and tidy, and if someone comes along and messes things up, I will scold them.

In conclusion, I am very happy that I am a Virgo. My patience and ambition gave me the confidence I needed to choose to be a psychologist. Because I work hard and can deal with people who have problems, I think I will someday be very successful in this profession. Some people envy me for the traits I have, and that gives me an idea that I am not so bad after all.

Organizing

The Example Essay

The student essay on page 61 is an example essay. Each paragraph gives an example to support the thesis statement.

To give examples, the following transitions can be used at the beginning of your paragraphs.

For the first body paragraph of your example essay:

> **One example of** [noun phrase] is . . .
>
> or
>
> Take, **for example,** . . .
>
> or
>
> **An example of** [noun phrase] is . . .

For the second paragraph of your example essay:

> **Another example of** [noun phrase] is . . .
>
> or
>
> **An additional example** is . . .
>
> or
>
> **A second example** of [noun phrase] is . . .

For the last paragraph of your example essay:

> **A final example** of [noun phrase] is . . .
>
> **Finally,** . . .

If your last example is the most important:

> The **most important example** of [noun phrase] is . . .
>
> The **most significant/interesting example** of [noun phrase] is . . .

Now underline the transitions used to introduce examples in the body paragraphs of the student essay.

In your body paragraphs, you may use other specific examples to support your topic sentence. The following words and phrases introduce examples:

> **For example,** . . .
>
> or
>
> **For instance,** . . .

For example and **for instance** have the same meaning. When your sentence begins with **for example** or **for instance,** put a comma after these words. Remember that when **for example** or **for instance** comes at the beginning of a sentence, it must be followed by a complete sentence.

> **For example,** it helps me to study when the lesson is difficult.
> **For instance,** I like everything to be neat and tidy.

Sometimes **e.g.** is used to show examples; it is an abbreviation of the Latin *exempli gratia*. **For example** and **e.g.** have the same meaning. Note the punctuation with **e.g.**

> I am very patient with people, too, **e.g.,** children and senior citizens.
> or
> I am very patient with people, too, **for example,** children and senior citizens.

When **for example, for instance,** or **e.g.** is used in the middle of a sentence, use commas before and after these words.

> For further examples, you may use **also** or **another.**

Exercise 1

Complete the following with the correct transitions. There may be more than one correct answer.

The left and right sides of the face are quite different. Each side shows different aspects of our personality. The left side of the face reveals the instinctive and hereditary aspects of our personality. When we are under stress, _____, with feelings like fear, anger, or even intense happiness, force is put on the muscles of the left side of the face. When we examine the left side of the face, our well-being and troubles show up more. _____, wrinkles on this side show the strong emotions we have experienced in our lives. The right side of the face reflects our intelligence and self-control. This side of the face is usually more relaxed and smoother. That is why, _____, movie stars prefer to have this side of their face photographed.

Writing Practice

Choose one of the following topics.

1. Describe some of your good and/or bad traits. Give specific examples of these traits.

2. Describe yourself according to the characteristics of your astrological sign.

3. Describe a person you know or would like to know, using examples of two or three character traits.

4. Describe the character of a famous person, using examples of his or her dominant character traits.

1. **Pre-writing.**

Work with a partner, a group, or alone.

a. Brainstorm the topic. Look at page 208 to find out about brainstorming. Choose one of the pre-writing brainstorming techniques that you prefer.

b. Brainstorm for ideas about strong character traits.

c. Work on a thesis statement.

2. **Outlining.**

a. Organize your ideas.

Step 1: Write your thesis statement.

Step 2: Pick the best examples of strong character traits.

Step 3: Remember to begin each paragraph with a transition showing example.

b. Make a more detailed outline. The essay outline on page 22 will help you.

3. **Write a rough draft.**

4. **Revise your rough draft.**

Using the checklist below, check your rough draft or let your partner check it.

Essay Checklist

Essay Organization

Introduction: _____ Does it include general statements?

_____ Is there a thesis statement?

Body: _____ Are there two or three paragraphs, each about a character trait?

_____ Does each paragraph begin with a transition showing example?

Conclusion: _____ Does it summarize main points or state your thesis again in other words?

_____ Is there a final comment on the topic?

Paragraph Organization

Topic Sentences: _____ Does each body paragraph have a topic sentence with a controlling idea?

Supporting Sentences: _____ Is each paragraph about one main idea? Do your sentences support your topic sentence?

_____ Do you have specific factual details and examples to support what you stated?

5. **Edit your essay.**

Work with a partner or a teacher to edit your essay. Correct spelling, punctuation, vocabulary, and grammar. Focus on finding errors in spelling.

Example:

Error: A person's apearance reveals more than we realize. *sp*

Correct: A person's appearance reveals more than we realize.

When you find a mistake of this type you can mark it with the symbol "sp" (spelling). Look at page 207 for other symbols to use when editing your work.

6. **Write your final copy.**

CHAPTER SIX

The Many Faces of Medicine

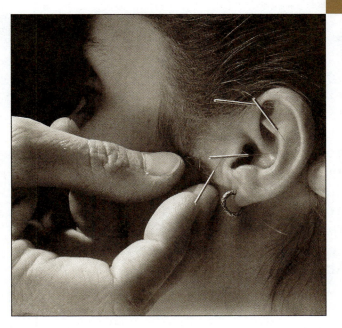

she is getting agrecculnture

needle

Pre-Reading Activity

Discuss these questions.

1. Why do you think the person in the picture has needles in her ear?
2. How would you feel if this were done to you?

Predicting

Answer the questions. Then compare your ideas with those in the reading.

◌ unusual(

1. What do you think is the main difference between alternative medicine and Western scientific medicine?
2. How many approaches to medicine do you know of?

Reflexology
Aromatherapy

The Many Faces of Medicine

anecdote method [handwritten]

interesting introduction [handwritten]

"**D**octor, I'm coughing and sneezing. I have itchy eyes, a drippy nose, and I ache all over. What's wrong with me? What should I do?"

"Take two aspirin and go to bed," one doctor advises.

"No, no. Drink this herbal tea," says another.

"Don't listen to them," argues the acupuncturist. "Come here and let me put some needles in your back."

Thesis statement [handwritten]

Who has the best remedy? All of them, some people would say, because they believe that there is more than one **approach** to healing and many ways to practice medicine. *topic* *controlling idea* [handwritten]

In general, modern medicine treats the body as if it were a machine made up of many separate parts that can break down **independently.** Treatment usually consists of trying to repair the broken part with drugs or surgery.

(Holistic doctors take another approach. They believe that the parts of the body are interconnected and must be treated as a whole. For example, to treat a headache, these doctors might recommend massage to relax the body, get the blood flowing, and **relieve** the **tension** that is causing the headache.)

Medical **practices** that do not depend on surgery and pharmaceutical drugs are called alternative forms of medicine. Some of these are more highly **respected** than others. For example, the Chinese method of acupuncture, although 2,000 years old, is considered an effective remedy for **chronic** pain. On the other hand, the practice of reflexology, which uses foot massage to heal other parts of the body, might feel good, but there is little proof that it works.)

Some forms of alternative medicine are centuries old. African herbalists have a long history of using tree bark, roots, grasses, and flowers to make teas to treat disease. Native Americans have used plant products to treat such illnesses as high blood pressure and coughs. At first, modern scientists laughed at herbal healers and called their methods "grandmother's remedies." Today, however, researchers are testing certain elements in plants for the possible treatment of cancer and AIDS.

Treatments that are unconventional, or out of the ordinary, have gained so much **prestige** and attention that the U.S. government has created an Office of Alternative Medicine. Researchers in this office study alternative forms of medicine in the United States and around the world. These include meditation, biofeedback, acupuncture, herbal medicine, hypnotism, homeopathy, and chiropractic medicine. In biofeedback, a machine is used to measure skin temperature and other responses. By watching the machine, a patient can learn to control muscle tension and blood pressure. Amazing results have come from the use of biofeedback, which has been successful in treating headaches, muscle pain, and even drug addiction. Homeopaths treat disease by giving a patient tiny amounts of a remedy that would produce symptoms similar to those of the disease in a healthy person. In Europe, this treatment has been known to help patients with flu, headaches, and allergies. People with back and muscle pain have been going to chiropractors for years, but it is only recently that chiropractors have received any kind of respect or recognition.

Many people have lost faith in modern medicine because researchers have been unable to find cures for a variety of problems, from cancer to the common cold. Some people turn to alternative medicine out of curiosity, others out of **desperation.** What many have realized is that often one treatment picks up where another leaves off. One medical technique can **complement** another. It seems likely that in the future the practice of medicine will consist of a combination of approaches drawn from a variety of cultures. We can hope that this approach will prove to be the best one of all.

Vocabulary

Meaning

What are the meanings of the underlined words? Circle the letter of each correct answer.

1. There is more than one <u>approach to</u> healing and many ways to practice medicine.

   a. idea of   c. discussion of
   b. method for   d. explanation of

2. Modern medicine treats the body as if it were a machine made up of many parts that can break down <u>independently</u>.
   a. slowly   c. together
   b. separately   d. easily

3. A headache may be treated with massage to <u>relieve</u> the tension causing the headache.
   a. test   c. prevent
   b. replace   d. decrease

4. A massage relaxes the body and relieves the <u>tension</u> that is causing the headaches.
   a. tightness   c. problem
   b. anger   d. muscle

5. Medical <u>practices</u> that do not depend on surgery and pharmaceutical drugs are called alternative forms of medicine.
   a. manners   c. theories
   b. habits   d. methods

6. Some forms of alternative medicine are more highly <u>respected</u> than others.
   a. admired   c. required
   b. controlled   d. encouraged

7. Acupuncture has been proved to be a very effective remedy for <u>chronic</u> pain.
   a. serious   c. long-lasting
   b. changing   d. extreme

8. Treatments that are unconventional have gained much <u>prestige</u> and attention.
   a. use   c. profit
   b. importance   d. evidence

9. Some turn to alternative medicine out of curiosity, others out of <u>desperation</u>.
   (a.) hopelessness   c.   lack of ability
   b.   careful thought   d.   fear

10. One medical technique can <u>complement</u> another.
   (a) add to   c.   take from
   b.   stay with   d.   contradict

Word Building

Complete the sentences with the correct form of the word in capital letters. You may use your dictionary.

1. EFFECT
   a.   Modern Western medicine can have unpleasant side _effect_.
   b.   In China, acupuncture has been found to be _effectione_ for centuries.

2. SUCCEED
   a.   Biofeedback methods have been _succeed_ in treating headache and muscle pain.
   b.   The vaccine has been working _succesfully_ for the last ten years.

3. PROVE
   a.   There is little _proof_ that reflexology works.
   b.   It is difficult to _prove_ how herbal medicine cures illnesses.

Comprehension

Looking for the Main Ideas

Circle the letter of the best answer.

1. Medicine is a science that _____.
   a.   can be practiced in more than one way
   b.   should never be changed
   c.   always uses surgery and drugs to heal people
   d.   can cure every illness

2. Traditional medical doctors and holistic doctors _____.

   a. both treat the body as if it were a machine made up of independent parts

   b. both use drugs and surgery

   c. have very different approaches to practicing medicine

   d. have lost faith in modern medicine

3. In the future, doctors will probably _____.

   a. stop using pharmaceutical drugs

   b. use machines to treat disease

   c. use several methods of treatment

   d. find drugs to cure all diseases

Looking for Details

Scan the reading quickly to find the answers to these questions. Write complete answers.

1. What approach do holistic doctors take to healing the body?

   _____

   _____

2. Give two examples of the use of alternative medicine.

   _____ Chinea Africa _____

   _____

3. Name two forms of alternative medicine that are highly respected.

   _____

   _____

4. Name one form of medicine for which we do not have proof that it works.

   _____

   _____

5. List three things that African herbalists use to make medicine.

_____ tree bark   roots   grasses _____

_____ flowers. _____

6. For approximately how long have the Chinese been practicing acupuncture?

_____ 2000 years _____

_____

7. Name five treatments being studied by researchers at the U.S. government's Office of Alternative Medicine.

_____

_____

8. Explain how biofeedback works.

_____

_____

Making Inferences and Drawing Conclusions

The answers to these questions are not directly stated in the reading. Write complete answers.

1. Why might someone turn to alternative medicine?

_____

_____

2. Why have unconventional forms of medicine gained prestige?

_____

_____

3. How might a holistic doctor treat a patient with an ulcer?

_____

_____

4. Why are some forms of alternative medicine more respected than others?

_____

_____

5. Why might conventional doctors be suspicious of alternative medicine?

_____

_____

Discussion

Discuss these questions with your classmates.

1. What form of medicine does your doctor practice?
2. Which forms of medicine mentioned in the reading would you like to try, and why?
3. Do you think a combination of different approaches to medicine is a good idea?
4. What do you think a doctor's office will look like in the future?

laryngitis

Organizing

Using *such as*

One way to introduce an example is by the use of **such as.** We use **such as** + example when we wish to be brief.

Examples:

Not at the first of sentences

Practices **such as** acupuncture are common in holistic medicine.
Some forms of alternative medicine, **such as** herbal healing, are centuries old.

Note: No commas are needed when the **such as** phrase gives essential information. Use commas when the **such as** phrase can be taken out without changing the meaning of the sentence.

, such as

Exercise 1

Combine the two sentences into one sentence using **such as.** Use correct punctuation. The first one is done for you.

1. Some uses of biofeedback have been successful. For instance, the treatments for headaches, muscle pain, and drug addiction have been successful.

   Some uses of biofeedback, such as the treatments of headaches, muscle pain, and drug addiction, have been successful.

2. African herbalists use parts of a tree to make teas. For example, African herbalists use the bark to make teas.

   African herbalists use parts of a tree, such as the bark, to mak teas.

3. Some forms of alternative medicine are highly respected. For example, the practice of acupuncture is highly respected.

Some forms of alternative medicine, such as the parctice of acupuncture, are highly respected.

4. There are many forms of alternative medicine from among which researchers today can choose. Herbal medicine, homeopathy, and chiropractic medicine are some examples.

5. Some practices feel good, but there is little proof that they work. An example of this type of practice is reflexology.

6. Homeopathy helps patients. For example, it helps patients with problems such as headaches and allergies.

Exercise 2

Punctuate these sentences containing examples, where necessary.

1. Homeopathy, for instance, is a type of alternative medicine.

2. Biofeedback is successful in treating the following: headaches, muscle pain, and even drug addiction.

3. For instance, they might use massage to treat a headache.

4. Chiropractic medicine is particularly helpful for treating problems such as back pain and muscle pain.

5. As an example, chicken soup is a familiar grandmother's remedy for *essay ← e.g. E.g. EX outline* a cold in the United States.

6. In some European countries, e.g., France, homeopathy is popular. *example*

Writing Practice

Choose one of the following topics.

1. Choose two natural products (e.g., garlic and ginseng) and give examples of problems they can be used to treat.
2. Give examples of how a health problem can be treated in two or more different ways.
3. Describe two or three "grandmother's remedies." Tell what they are used for and whether they work.

1. **Pre-writing.**

    Work with a partner, a group, or alone.

    a. Brainstorm the topic. Choose a pre-writing brainstorming technique that you prefer. (See page 208.)
    b. Work on a thesis statement.

2. **Outlining.**

    a. Organize your ideas.
        Step 1: Write your thesis statement.
        Step 2: Pick the two or three best examples from your brainstorming activity.
        Step 3: Remember to use a variety of words and phrases to show examples.
    b. Make a more detailed outline.

3. **Write a rough draft.**

4. Revise your rough draft.

Using the checklist below, check your rough draft or let your partner check it.

Essay Checklist

Essay Organization

Introduction:	_____	Does it include general statements?
	_____	Is there a thesis statement?
Body:	_____	Does each body paragraph give a clear example of a product or remedy?
	_____	Are transitions used to show examples?
Conclusion:	_____	Does it summarize main points or state your thesis again in other words?
	_____	Is there a final comment on the topic?

Paragraph Organization

Topic Sentences:	_____	Does each body paragraph have a topic sentence with a controlling idea?
Supporting Sentences:	_____	Is each paragraph about one main idea? Do your sentences support your topic sentence?
	_____	Do you have specific details or examples to support what you have stated?

5. Edit your essay.

Work with a partner or a teacher to edit your essay. Correct spelling, punctuation, vocabulary, and grammar. Focus on finding errors in subject/verb agreement. Remember that the subject and the verb must agree in person and in number.

Example:

Error: The number of famous people who are lefthanded <u>are</u>   *sv*
        amazing.
Correct: The number of famous people who are lefthanded is
        amazing.

When you find a mistake of this type, you can mark it with the symbol "sv" (subject/verb). Look at page 207 for other symbols to use when editing your work.

6. Write your final copy.

Do you know these facts about your body?

Circle the letter of the best answer.

1. How long does it take for the blood to circulate throughout the body when you rest?

    a. two minutes

    b. sixty seconds

    c. forty seconds

2. The body burns calories fastest when you exercise within _____.

    a. three hours after a meal

    b. six hours after a meal

    c. eight hours after you sleep

3. When you smoke a cigarette, the nicotine in the tobacco reaches the brain in _____.

    a. one minute

    b. fifteen seconds

    c. seven seconds

4. We lose an eyelash every _____.

    a. three to five months

    b. six to eight months

    c. one to two weeks

5. Your gums are renewed every _____.

    a. six to eight months

    b. three to five years

    c. one to two weeks

6. Fingernails grow _____.

    a. as fast as toenails

    b. four times as fast as toenails

    c. twice as fast as toenails

Video Activity · Yoga for Health

1. The video is about yoga exercises. What is yoga? In what ways can it improve people's health?

2. As you watch the video, listen for the answers to the following questions. Put a check mark before the correct answers.

   a. How many million Americans practice yoga?

   _____ 3   _____ 6   _____ 8   _____ 10

   b. What are the parts of Hatha Yoga?
   _____ gentle poses   _____ weightlifting
   _____ breathing   _____ meditation

   c. Which diseases can yoga help with?
   _____ carpal tunnel syndrome   _____ diabetes
   _____ pneumonia   _____ arthritis

   d. What are two benefits of yoga mentioned in the video?
   _____ reduced stress   _____ better digestion
   _____ improved concentration

3. Discuss these questions: Do you practice yoga? If you don't, would you like to? What are some tips for practicing yoga? Does it have any risks? Make a list of tips for someone who wants to start learning yoga.

Internet Activity

- Look up "phrenology" on the Internet. Find out more about the history of phrenology. What other scientists were interested in phrenology? In which countries did it become popular?

- What were the sources of the web sites you visited? Which web site did you think was most reliable, and why?

People

CHAPTER SEVEN

The Shakers

Pre-Reading Activity

Discuss these questions.

1. Describe the picture. What country do you think it is?
2. Why do you think the people in the picture are dressed in this way?
3. Do you think men and women should live apart? Why or why not?

Predicting

Based on the picture above, complete the chart with information about the Shakers. Write one thing you know, one thing you are not sure about, and one thing you would like to find out about the Shakers. Then compare your ideas with those in the reading.

One thing I know	One thing I am not sure about	One thing I would like to find out

The Shakers

"**S**hake it up baby. Twist and shout," was sung by the Beatles, but it was practiced almost 200 years earlier by a religious group called "The United Society of Believers." This religious group was founded in England. In 1774, Shaker leader Ann Lee and her followers emigrated to America. The Believers worshipped by singing, dancing, shaking, and **whirling** around. Eventually they became known as "the Shakers."

The Shakers were a peaceful **sect** that welcomed people of all races. They were against war and lived in their own villages separate from the rest of society. They lived communally—that is, sharing their property and working for the common good. The qualities they admired were kindness, generosity, modesty, purity, cleanliness, and love for humanity. Their villages of plain white houses were so neat and tidy that even the roads were swept clean.

The Shakers were probably best known for their **celibacy** and **industriousness.** Single men and women did not marry. Married couples who joined the religion had to live apart. In the Shaker community, males and females lived in separate communal houses. They had strict rules regarding behavior between the sexes, such as never shaking hands or touching each other in any way. They ate, worked, and slept in separate **quarters.** When conversation between a man and a woman was necessary, it was done in the company of others. At their almost daily meetings for conversation and singing, males and females sat opposite each other. Even when they danced and whirled around during worship, men and women always kept their distance.

As might be expected, the Shaker style of dressing was modest, simple, and plain, and their clothes were dark in color. The women combed their hair back under a cap and wore long dresses with a cloth that covered the chest. Men wore dark pants and simple coats. Bright or attractive clothing was out of the question for these celibate people.

"Put your hands to work and your hearts to God," said Ann Lee to her followers. Those words were taken seriously by the Shakers, who were very hardworking people. In order to be **self-sufficient,** the

Shakers grew their own food, wove their own cloth, and made their own tools, utensils, and handicrafts. They made chairs, buttons, tubs, baskets, smoking pipes, pens, brooms, brushes, hats, shoes, and hand-woven coats. Although simple and plain, these things were of the highest quality, and the Shakers soon became famous for their superior products.

Not only were the Shakers industrious, but they were creative and inventive as well. Their long list of inventions and improvements includes such items as the flat broom, the common clothespin, the first garden seeds packaged in paper, and machines such as an improved washing machine, a revolving oven, and a wood-burning stove.

Although it may seem that Shaker life was all rules, work, and worship, their lives were not without joy. They spent pleasant hours gathering berries and picking fruit, walking in the woods, taking carriage rides, and laughing together—in separate groups, of course.

Over the years, the original Shaker community in New York expanded to 24 communities **scattered** among eight states in the eastern United States. Many people were attracted to their peaceful ways and clean, crime-free villages. Eventually the Shakers paid a price for their celibacy, however, because without children to carry on their traditions and beliefs, their numbers eventually **dwindled** to a very few. Today, their villages are museums and their handicrafts are items for collectors. Nevertheless, the Shakers will not be forgotten. Their search for a perfect existence where everyone was equal and lived in **harmony** is recorded in American history. The Shakers will be remembered for their many fine products and inventions and for the **contribution** they made to society.

Vocabulary

Meaning

What are the meanings of the underlined words? Circle the letter of each correct answer.

1. The Shakers worshipped by dancing, shaking, and <u>whirling</u> around.
   a. rolling
   c. jumping
   b. turning
   d. falling

2. The Shakers were a peaceful <u>sect</u>.
    a. group of people with special religious beliefs
    b. group of people belonging to a secret organization
    c. group of people belonging to a political party
    d. group of people from one country

3. The Shakers were known for their <u>celibacy</u>.
    a. marrying many times
    b. having large families
    c. not marrying because of religious beliefs
    d. living alone

4. The Shakers were also known for their <u>industriousness</u>.
    a. hard work   c. businessmindedness
    b. laziness   d. imagination

5. Shaker men and women ate, worked, and slept in separate <u>quarters</u>.
    a. living areas   c. villages
    b. gardens   d. groups

6. The Shakers were almost totally <u>self-sufficient</u>.
    a. able to grow fruit and vegetables
    b. able to provide for their own needs without outside help
    c. able to keep alive on very little food
    d. able to trade goods with other people

7. The Shaker communities expanded from the original one to 24 communities <u>scattered</u> among eight states.
    a. covered up   c. spread out
    b. grouped together   d. joined up

8. Eventually the Shakers <u>dwindled</u> in number.
    a. gradually became fewer   c. suddenly disappeared
    b. gradually increased   d. suddenly multiplied

9. In the Shaker community, everyone was equal and lived in
   harmony.
   a. melody   c. groups
   b. agreement with one another   d. isolation

10. The Shakers will be remembered for the contribution they made to
    society.
    a. problem   c. protest
    b. money   d. gift

Word Building

Complete the sentences with the correct form of the word in capital
letters. You may use your dictionary.

1. CREATE
   a. The Shakers were _____ as well as hardworking.
   b. They _____ many useful objects.

2. KIND
   a. The qualities of _____ and generosity were important to
      the Shakers.
   b. They tried to be _____ to others.

3. INVENT
   a. The Shakers were very _____ people.
   b. They thought of many new _____ for the home.

Comprehension

Looking for the Main Ideas

Circle the letter of the correct answer.

1. The Shakers were _____.
    a. a religious group whose main belief was shaking
    b. a peaceful sect that lived communally
    c. not a true religious sect
    d. a religious group that did not welcome others

2. The Shakers were known for their _____.
    a. farming methods
    b. decorated houses
    c. songs and traditions
    d. celibacy and hard work

3. Today, the Shakers _____.
    a. have dwindled in number to a few
    b. make handicrafts for museums
    c. have increased in number and live in villages that have become museums
    d. no longer exist

Looking for Details

Scan the reading quickly to find the answers to these questions. Write complete answers.

1. Who brought the Shakers to America?

    _____

    _____

2. What qualities did the Shakers admire?

    _____

    _____

3. Under what conditions could a man have a conversation with a woman in the Shaker community?

_____

_____

4. What did a Shaker man wear?

_____

_____

5. What are some of the machines the Shakers invented?

_____

_____

6. What did the Shakers do for fun?

_____

_____

Making Inferences and Drawing Conclusions

The answers to these questions are not directly stated in the reading. Write complete sentences.

1. What would happen to a married couple with a child who joined the Shaker community?

_____

_____

2. Why do you think people joined the Shakers?

_____

_____

3. Why do you think they made such high-quality products?

_____

_____

4. Why did the Shakers want to be self-sufficient?

_____

_____

5. Why didn't the Shakers wear fashionable, colorful clothes?

_____

_____

Discussion

Discuss these questions with your classmates.

1. What other religious or nonreligious communities have you heard about?
2. Why do you think people are happy living in these communities?
3. Would you like to live in a special community? If so, what idea would you want it to be based on?
4. Celibacy and industriousness were important characteristics of the Shakers. Do you think these are positive qualities? Why or why not?
5. Name a positive quality in a person. Explain why you think it is good.
6. Name a negative quality in a person. Explain why it is bad.

Read the following essay written by a student. Underline the thesis statement and the topic sentence in each of the body paragraphs.

Model Essay

My Cousin Patricia

My cousin Patricia is a teacher and works for Santa Maria de Fatima High School, in Peru. She has been teaching there for the last six years. She is 32, but looks much younger. Patty is a very nice person to get along with and has some very good qualities.

Patricia believes all people are equal. She likes to show people that women as well as men can do anything and be successful. When she talks about current events, she likes to mention the achievements of men and women of all races and nations. She often asks her students to do research on organizations in which people work together to make the world a better place.

My cousin is a good leader. If you ever had a chance to join any of her group meetings, you would notice right away how she enjoys leading others while encouraging them to participate in what is going on. When there are decisions to be made, she listens to everyone's opinions and respects everyone's suggestions. People who know that aspect of her like her very much. People like to be with her, and she has many friends. The only thing bad I can say about her is that I don't see her often enough.

In conclusion, my cousin Patty is very nice in many ways, is a very good teacher, and is the best company a person could have. I wish she didn't live so far away, but someday maybe she will come to live near my family. That will be a wonderful day.

final thought

Organizing

The Dominant Impression

Often when describing people we use the <u>dominant impression</u>. The *dominant impression* is the main effect a person has on our feelings or senses. We give the dominant impression by selecting the most important feature or character trait of a person and emphasizing it. Adjectives like *shy, beautiful, ambitious,* or *generous* can easily give a dominant impression. This impression is then supported by details.

The first topic sentence in a paragraph will usually give you the dominant impression. Look at the student essay and underline the words in the topic sentence of each body paragraph that give you the dominant impression.

Exercise 1

Look at each dominant impression and the group of sentences below it. In each case, find the sentences that do not support the dominant impression.

1. Dominant impression: My brother is <u>ambitious</u>.
    a. He likes to watch the latest news on television.
    b. He takes extra classes at school.
    c. He's captain of his football team.
    d. He's already decided that he wants to be a doctor.
    e. He takes a trip to Switzerland every year.

2. Dominant impression: My best friend is <u>shy</u>.
    a. She never speaks to people when there's a party.
    b. She likes to read books a lot.
    c. She never raises her voice.
    d. She likes to wear green sweaters.
    e. She always disappears when I want to introduce her to someone.

3. Dominant impression: My aunt is <u>thoughtful</u>.

    a. She always remembers my birthday.

    b. She likes to work in the garden.

    c. She likes to listen to classical music and read poetry.

    d. She always offers me a cup of tea when I visit.

    e. She offers me a sweater when I'm cold.

Writing Practice

Choose one of the following topics.

1. Describe yourself or someone you know, using one or two adjectives to give the dominant impression.

2. Describe a group of people, a race, or a nation, using one or two adjectives stereotyping the dominant impression.

1. Pre-writing.

Work with a partner, a group, or alone.

a. Brainstorm the topic. Choose a pre-writing brainstorming technique that you prefer. (See page 208.)

b. Brainstorm descriptive adjectives and supporting details for them.

c. Work on a thesis statement.

2. Outlining.

a. Organize your ideas.

Step 1: Write your thesis statement.

Step 2: Pick one or two of the best descriptive adjectives from your brainstorming activity.

Step 3: Remember to find relevant details to support your dominant impression.

b. Make a more detailed outline. The essay outline on page 22 will help you.

3. Write a rough draft.

4. Revise your rough draft.

    Using the checklist below, check your rough draft or let your partner check it.

    ### Essay Checklist

    Essay Organization

Introduction:	____	Does it include general statements?
	____	Is there a thesis statement?
Body:	____	Are the descriptive details in a logical sequence?
	____	Do you establish a point of view, either first person (I, we) or third person (he, she, they), and keep to the same point of view throughout?
Conclusion:	____	Does it summarize main points or state your thesis again in other words?
	____	Is there a final comment on the topic?

    Paragraph Organization

Topic Sentences:	____	Does each body paragraph have a topic sentence with a controlling idea?
Supporting Sentences:	____	Is each paragraph about one main idea? Do your sentences support your topic sentence?
	____	Do you have specific details to support what you have said?

5. Edit your essay.

    Work with a partner or a teacher to edit your essay. Correct spelling, punctuation, vocabulary, and grammar. Read your rough draft and try to find errors in capitalization.

    ### Example:

    Error: The shakers were a <u>R</u>eligious group originating from   lc
    <u>m</u>anchester in <u>e</u>ngland.   cap
    Correct: The Shakers were a religious group originating from Manchester in England.

    When you find a mistake of this type, you can mark it with the symbol "cap" or "lc" (capital or lower case). Look at page 207 for other symbols you can use when editing your work.

6. Write your final copy.

CHAPTER EIGHT

George Washington Carver

Pre-Reading Activity

Discuss these questions.

1. George Washington Carver was a famous African American scientist. What other famous scientists do you know of?

2. What problems do you think Carver had because he was African American?

3. What other famous African Americans do you know of?

Predicting

The following words are taken from the story of George Washington Carver. Try to guess how each of these words plays a part in his story. Then compare your ideas with those in the reading.

painting	farming	postage stamps
ironing	experiments	

George Washington Carver

George Washington Carver, who was born a slave in 1861, became one of America's greatest scientists in the **field** of **agriculture.** His discoveries changed farming in the South of the United States. A quiet and kind man, he could have become rich from his discoveries but preferred "to be of the greatest good to the greatest number of my people."

George's mother was a slave, but soon after he was born, he and his brother lost their mother and became **orphans.** They were raised by Moses and Susan Carver, who were their owners. Slaves took the names of their owners, so George Washington's last name was Carver, too. In 1865, there were no longer slaves in the United States, but George and his brother continued to live with the Carvers. The Carvers gave him as much of an education as they could. At age 12, George left the Carvers to start life on his own.

For the next 12 years, he worked whenever he could and went to school whenever he could. He managed to finish high school and won a scholarship to go to Highland University. However, when he appeared at the university, they refused **to admit** him because he was black. This did not stop Carver. He continued to work and save money. Eventually, he went to Simpson College in 1890 to study painting and paid for his school by ironing clothes for other students. Soon, he realized he could not **support himself** as an artist and decided to study agriculture instead.

In 1891, he was accepted at Iowa Agricultural College. He was the only black student at the college, and as usual he supported himself by doing small jobs. He amazed everyone with his special work with plants. After he graduated, the college asked him to stay on as an instructor because his work with plants and chemistry was so **outstanding.** So Carver stayed on and taught, but he continued his research with plants while he was teaching.

One day he received a letter from Booker T. Washington, who was the most respected black educator in the country. Washington asked him to work at the Tuskegee Institute, a black agricultural school in

Alabama. Tuskegee was a poor black school that could not give Carver a laboratory or a high salary, but Carver decided to go there.

In 1896, Carver started to teach and do research with plants at the Tuskegee Institute. He taught classes on agriculture, and through his experiments he found new ways to help the poor, **struggling** farmers of the South. Here, farmers had been growing cotton, which **wore out** the **soil.** He showed farmers how to plant different crops like peanuts to make the soil richer. After a while, farmers did what he said and were growing more and more peanuts. They were now making more money from peanuts than from cotton.

Carver developed many uses for the peanut. In fact, he found more than 300 uses for the peanut, and he became known as the "peanut man." He received many prizes and awards for his work. He gave lectures about the uses of peanuts all over the United States and even spoke to Congress about peanuts in 1921. Meanwhile, Carver began to experiment with the sweet potato and discovered more than 100 products that could be made from it, including glue for postage stamps.

By the 1930s, Carver had become famous all over the country and the world. He visited the Prince of Sweden and the British Prince of Wales. Thomas Edison asked Carver to work for him at a salary of more than $100,000 a year. The car manufacturer Henry Ford also made him a generous **offer.** But Carver was not interested in money; he stayed on at the Tuskegee Institute with a monthly salary of $125.

In 1940, he gave all his life savings of $33,000 to the George Washington Carver Foundation **to provide opportunities for** African Americans to study in his field, because for Carver, "Education is the key to unlock the golden door of freedom. . . ." Carver died in 1943.

Vocabulary

Meaning

What are the meanings of the underlined words? Circle the letter of each correct answer.

1. George Washington Carver was a famous man in his <u>field</u>.
   a. area of grassland
   c. area where he lived
   b. area of interest or study
   d. a slave all his life

2. Carver's interest was <u>agriculture</u>.
   a. describing plants
   c. painting flowers
   b. cleaning animals
   d. growing food

3. Carver was <u>an orphan</u>.
   a. a child who has no mother and no father
   b. a child who has one brother
   c. a child who has just a mother
   d. a child who has no brothers or sisters

4. The university didn't <u>admit</u> Carver.
   a. allow to enter
   c. recognize
   b. allow to apply
   d. respect

5. It is hard to <u>support yourself</u> as an artist.
   a. be strong
   c. earn enough money to live
   b. have confidence
   d. get help

6. Carver's work was <u>outstanding</u>.
   a. better than most
   c. permanent
   b. different
   d. strange

7. Carver wanted to help <u>struggling</u> farmers.
   a. uneducated
   c. hardworking
   b. religious
   d. trying to survive

8. Farmers grew cotton on the <u>soil</u>.
   a. part of the land by the water
   b. dirt in which plants grow
   c. land that people don't want
   d. dirt of poor quality

9. Cotton <u>wore out</u> the land.
   a. covered
   c. used up
   b. helped
   d. poisoned

10. Henry Ford <u>made him an offer</u>.

    a.   proposed something to him

    b.   sold him something

    c.   rewarded him with a prize

    d.   gave him a gift of money

11. Carver wanted to <u>provide opportunities for</u> African Americans.

    a.   give hope to   c.   wish good luck to

    b.   give a chance to   d.   be an example to

Word Building

Complete the sentences with the correct form of the word in capital letters. You may use your dictionary.

1. WEAR

    a.   The soil was _____ out from overfarming cotton.

    b.   Carver introduced plants that didn't _____ out the soil.

2. DISCOVER

    a.   Carver _____ many uses for peanuts.

    b.   His _____ changed farming methods in the South.

3. AGRICULTURE

    a.   Carver studied at the _____ College.

    b.   He did research on new methods of _____.

Comprehension

Looking for the Main Ideas

Circle the letter of the best answer.

1. Carver was _____.

    a.   born a slave

    b.   a slave until he was 12

    c.   a slave until he went to the university

    d.   a slave all his life

2. Carver developed many uses for _____ .
    a. cotton   c. glue
    b. peanuts   d. soil

3. In the 1930s, Carver was _____ .
    a. a poor and unrecognized man
    b. a rich and recognized man
    c. not famous in other countries
    d. recognized all over the world

Looking for Details

Circle T if the sentence is true. Circle F if the sentence is false. Correct the false sentences.

1. George's parents were Moses and Susan Carver.   T   F

2. Carver was the only black student at Iowa
    Agricultural College.   T   F

3. Booker T. Washington wrote Carver a letter.   T   F

4. Carver was called the "peanut man."   T   F

5. Carver discovered more than 300 products for the
    sweet potato.   T   F

6. Henry Ford offered Carver $100,000 a year to work
    for him.   T   F

7. Carver gave his life savings to the George Washington
    Carver Foundation after he died.   T   F

Making Inferences and Drawing Conclusions

The answers to these questions are not directly stated in the reading. Write complete sentences.

1. What kind of slave owners were Moses and Susan Carver?

    _____

    _____

2. Why did Carver go from place to place for 12 years or more of his life?

_____

_____

3. Why was it difficult for Carver to get an education?

_____

_____

4. Why did Booker T. Washington ask him to work at the Tuskegee Institute?

_____

_____

5. Why did Carver decide to go to work at the Tuskegee Institute?

_____

_____

6. How did Carver's discoveries change farming in the South?

_____

_____

Discussion

Discuss these questions with your classmates.
1. Carver loved his work, but he did not care about money. Is this good or bad? Why?
2. What kind of person do you have to be to come up with new ideas?
3. What other famous people do you know of who have risen from difficult beginnings?
4. Who are some famous people who have helped others?

Organizing

The story of George Washington Carver is a narrative. A *narrative* relates a story of events or actions. Narrative puts events in time and tells us what happened according to a natural time sequence.

In a narrative, time order words and phrases are used to show the order in which events happen.

first (second, etc.)	eventually
then	when
next	a few days later
finally	one day
after, afterward	after a while
meanwhile	in 1940
soon	for the next [number] years

Note: Time order words and phrases at the beginning of a sentence are followed by a comma.

Look back at the reading and underline all the time order words and phrases in the story of George Washington Carver.

Exercise 1

The sentences about George Washington Carver (below and on the next page) are not in the correct time order. Number the sentences in the correct order.

_____ Carver finished high school.

_____ George Washington Carver was born a slave in 1861.

_____ Carver went to Iowa Agricultural College.

_____ He received a letter from Booker T. Washington offering him a job at the Tuskegee Institute in Alabama.

_____ He continued to live with his former owners until he was 12.

_____ He went to Simpson College but soon left.

_____ He stayed on and became an instructor at Iowa Agricultural College.

_____ Carver developed many uses for the peanut.

_____ He became famous all over the world.

_____ Before he died, he gave his life savings to the George Washington Carver Foundation.

_____ He graduated from Iowa Agricultural College.

_____ Carver started to work at the Tuskegee Institute.

_____ Carver spoke to Congress about peanuts.

Using Description with Narrative

Often, we do not use one form of writing alone. For example, a story, which is usually a narrative, will have descriptions of people and places. Here are some examples of description from the George Washington Carver story.

Examples:

He was a quiet and kind man.
He found new ways to help poor, struggling farmers.
His work with plants and chemistry was outstanding.

We use _adjectives_ to describe people and places. Adjectives modify nouns. They come before nouns, but they come after some verbs like _be, become,_ and _get._

He was a   <u>quiet</u>   and   <u>kind</u>   <u>man</u>.
      (Adjective)   (Adjective) (Noun)

He found new ways to help   <u>poor,</u>   <u>struggling</u> <u>farmers</u>.
                  (Adjective) (Adjective)   (Noun)

His   <u>work</u>   was <u>outstanding</u>.
   (Noun)   (Adjective)

Underline all the adjectives in the reading. Then underline the nouns they modify twice.

Writing Practice

Choose one of the following topics.

1. Write the story of your life or the life of a person you know.
2. Write the story of a famous person.
3. Describe how someone influenced your life.

1. **Pre-writing.**

    Work with a partner, a group, or alone.

    a. Brainstorm the topic. Choose a pre-writing brainstorming technique that you prefer. (See page 208.)
    b. Write down important events in your or someone else's life.
    c. Work on a thesis statement.

2. **Outlining.**

    a. Organize your ideas.

    Step 1: Write your thesis statement.

    Step 2: Arrange the events in the correct order.

    Step 3: Decide whether you will tell the story in the first person (I, we) or in the third person (he, she, they). Remember to keep the same person throughout your story.

    b. Make a more detailed outline. Remember to use some description in your story.

3. **Write a rough draft.**

4. **Revise your rough draft.**

Using the checklist below, check your rough draft or let your partner check it.

Essay Checklist

Essay Organization

Introduction:	_____	Does it include general statements?
	_____	Is there a thesis statement?
Body:	_____	Are the events in a logical order?
	_____	Are time words used to show the order of events?
Conclusion:	_____	Does it tell the end of the story or the result of the events?

Paragraph Organization

Topic Sentences:	_____	Does each body paragraph show a sequence of events?
Supporting Sentences:	_____	Do your sentences describe or illustrate the events?
	_____	Do you have specific details to support what you have said?

5. **Edit your essay.**

Work with a partner or a teacher to edit your essay. Correct spelling, punctuation, vocabulary, and grammar. Read your rough draft and try to find errors in word formation.

Example:

Error: He was a very <u>carefully</u> researcher and scientist.   *wf*
Correct: He was a very careful researcher and scientist.

When you find a mistake of this type, you can mark it with the symbol "wf" (word form). Look at page 207 for other symbols to use when editing your work.

6. **Write your final copy.**

Do you know who they are?

Circle T if the sentence is true. Circle F if the sentence is false.

1. The first woman in space was an American, Sally Ride.   T   F

2. The largest manufacturer of sports clothes in the world,
    Adidas, was started by a German, Adolf Dasler, in the 1920s.   T   F

3. The gypsies, who today number 5 million people, originally
    came from Egypt.   T   F

4. Only three people have received Oscar nominations for both
    best screenwriter and best actor. The first was Charlie Chaplin,
    the second was Orson Welles, and the third was Sylvester
    Stallone.   T   F

5. David Attenborough invented the aqualung, produced
    the world's first underwater camera, and then started making
    underwater films for TV.   T   F

6. Seiji Ozawa is a world-famous conductor from Japan.   T   F

Video Activity • Harlem Photographer   CNN

1. Austen Hansen was a photographer who took many photographs in
    Harlem, New York. According to the video, what kind of photographs
    did he take? Check the types of photos that are shown or mentioned
    in the video.

    _____ politicians   _____ ordinary people   _____ war photos
    _____ buildings   _____ news photos   _____ paintings
    _____ sports events   _____ musicians

2. Complete the following sentences about Austen Hansen's life.

    a. He was born and grew up in _____.

    b. He immigrated to New York in _____ when he was 18.

    c. In New York, he played _____ in a band.

    d. Hansen served as _____ for a number of Harlem churches.

3. Work in a group of three or four students. What do you think
    motivated Austen Hansen to take photographs? What do you think of
    his photos? Work together to write a short news article about Austen
    Hansen's life.

Internet Activity

- Look up "Shakers" on the Internet. Where do they live today? Can you visit them? What kinds of occupations do they have?

- Compare two web sites containing information about the Shakers. Who created the web sites? What kind of information do they provide?

Food

CHAPTER NINE

A Variety of American Foods

Pre-Reading Activity

Discuss these questions.

1. Look at the two pictures and tell how they are different.
2. In what regions of the United States could you find each of these foods?
3. How might the lifestyles of people who live in these regions be different?

Predicting

Answer the questions. Then compare your ideas with those in the reading.

1. Name five of the most popular American foods.
2. What types of foods are eaten in different parts of the United States and why?

A Variety of American Foods

The French are famous for their sauces, the Italians are praised for their pasta, and the Germans are **celebrated** for their sausages, but is there anything unique to eat in the United States? When you get right down to it, there's nothing quite as un-American as American food. Because the United States is made up mostly of immigrants, there is an amazing variety of foods, from clam chowder in Boston to chile con carne in Houston. The United States is a vast country influenced by many cultures and climates, and the traditional food of one area is often totally unlike that of another. New Mexico and Massachusetts are good examples of states that have very different traditional foods.

To understand and appreciate the food in any one region, it often helps to know the area's history. For example, New Mexico was once the home of the Pueblo Indians, who lived in villages and grew native crops such as corn, beans, pumpkins, and squash. Later, Spanish settlers arrived in this area. These two groups exchanged ideas and customs and passed these customs on to their descendants. The intermingling of cultures is evident in the food of New Mexico.

New Mexican meals make much use of corn, which is served in a variety of ways—baked as tortillas, served fresh as **corn on the cob, blended** into soups and sauces, and mixed into salads or with other vegetables, especially red and green peppers. Native blue corn is quite surprising when it is served as blue corn bread, chips, or tortillas. In the markets of New Mexico, you can still find *chicos,* or sun-dried grains of roasted sweet corn. *Chicos* last a long time, but when **soaked** and boiled, they taste almost like fresh corn. Many recipes also contain *piñon,* or pine nuts, the small sweet seeds of the southwestern pine tree, once a **staple** food in the Pueblo diet.

A Spanish influence can be found in the sweet, anise-flavored cookies sold in New Mexico bakeries. They are prepared much as they were made in the kitchens of seventeenth-century Spain for the Christmas feast.

Some traditional foods of New Mexico that show both a native American and a Spanish **heritage** include enchiladas (corn tortillas

stuffed with cheese, onions, tomatoes, chilies, and sometimes chicken or beef), pinto beans, black beans, and hot and spicy salsa, an uncooked vegetable sauce.

Take a trip to Massachusetts, however, and not a chili pepper nor a tortilla will you find in a traditional meal. Influenced by the cold climate and the English-speaking people who settled there, the **New England** kitchen gives off the aromas of soups and stews and of meat that is roasted for hours in the oven. Potatoes, carrots, and turnips were popular, because these root vegetables grew well in the region and could be stored all winter long in the days before supermarkets and refrigerators. English-style puddings and pies are the traditional desserts, rather than the fresh fruit one often gets in the Southwest.

Whereas beef and chicken appear in many New Mexican recipes, in Massachusetts fish is very popular because of the nearby seacoast. New England is famous for its clam chowder, lobster, cod, scallops, and fish cakes. English herbs and spices are the seasonings used in New England dishes, which might taste rather **bland** to people accustomed to hot and spicy New Mexican food.

Each region of the United States is unique. Louisiana has a French influence. Many Germans populate the Midwest. In traveling around America, a tourist has the opportunity not only to visit a variety of places and see **diverse** landscapes, but to taste a variety of foods as well. Some may be very different. Others will taste just like home.

Vocabulary

Meaning

What are the meanings of the underlined words? Circle the letter of each correct answer.

1. The Germans are <u>celebrated</u> for their sausages.
   - a. appreciated
   - c. remembered
   - b. concerned
   - d. well known

2. <u>Corn on the cob</u> is served in New Mexico.
   - a. chopped corn
   - c. crushed corn
   - b. whole ears of corn
   - d. fresh corn

3. In New Mexico, corn is <u>blended</u> into soups.
   a. mixed
   c. drained
   b. poured
   d. chopped

4. When chicos are <u>soaked</u> and boiled, they taste like fresh corn.
   a. left in water
   c. dried in the sun
   b. cut into small pieces
   d. fried in oil

5. Pine nuts were a <u>staple</u> food in the Pueblo Indians' diet.
   a. popular
   c. unusual
   b. basic
   d. frequent

6. Some foods of New Mexico show both a native American and a Spanish <u>heritage</u>.
   a. flavor
   c. condition
   b. tradition
   d. recipe

7. Enchiladas are corn tortillas <u>stuffed</u> with cheese, onions, tomatoes, and chilies.
   a. melted
   c. filled
   b. eaten
   d. covered

8. The <u>New England</u> kitchen gives off the aromas of soups and stews.
   a. southwestern United States
   b. northeastern United States
   c. midwestern United States
   d. southern United States

9. New England food might taste rather <u>bland</u> to some people.
   a. tasteless
   c. flavorful
   b. spicy
   d. bitter

10. America has a <u>diverse</u> landscape.
    a. rough
    c. flat
    b. changing
    d. surprising

Word Building

Complete the sentences with the correct form of the word in capital letters. You may use your dictionary.

1. HISTORY
   a. There are often _____ reasons why certain foods are popular.
   b. The arrival of Spanish settlers in New Mexico was an important event in the _____ of the Southwest.

2. COOK
   a. Potatoes have to be _____ before we can eat them.
   b. The climate can have a great effect on the regional style of _____.

3. INFLUENCE
   a. There is a French _____ on the food in Louisiana.
   b. Spanish traditions have been _____ in the development of New Mexican cuisine.

Comprehension

Looking for the Main Ideas

Circle the letter of the best answer.

1. America _____.
   a. has lots of typical foods
   b. has not shared many customs with other people
   c. does not have its own traditional food
   d. has been influenced by many cultures

2. Food in America _____.
   a. is the same from coast to coast
   b. is mostly hot and spicy
   c. changes from one place to another
   d. reflects the character of the people

3. To appreciate the food in a region, _____.
   a. it helps to know the area's history
   b. it's important to see the landscape
   c. a tourist has to travel to many areas
   d. you have to learn the recipes

Looking for Details

Circle T if the sentence is true. Circle F if the sentence is false.

1. The Spanish settlers and Pueblo Indians in New Mexico
   shared their customs.   T   F

2. The Spanish brought corn to the Pueblo Indians.   T   F

3. Corn is served only on special occasions in New Mexico.   T   F

4. Lobster is a favorite dish in New Mexico.   T   F

5. In America, the traditional food of one area is often
   very different from that of another area.   T   F

6. Beef was a staple food of the native Americans.   T   F

7. Climate has an influence on the type of food eaten in
   certain areas.   T   F

8. Food in Louisiana has been influenced by the French.   T   F

9. New England is famous for its clam chowder.   T   F

10. Fresh fruit is popular only in the Northeast.   T   F

Making Inferences and Drawing Conclusions

The answers to these questions are not directly stated in the reading.
Write complete sentences.

1. Why are the foods in different regions of the United States so
   different?

   _____

   _____

2. How does the history of an area help us to appreciate the food that is eaten there?

_____

_____

3. Why is the food in New Mexico often hot and spicy?

_____

_____

4. Why do so many New England meals consist of hearty foods like stews and roasts and puddings and pies?

_____

_____

5. What kinds of food might a person find in the Midwest?

_____

_____

Discussion

Discuss these questions with your classmates.

1. Describe the similarities and differences between two or more regions in your country. (Are there differences in climate? In geography?)
2. Describe two types of cuisine in your country.
3. What do you think about food in America?
4. Compare breakfast in your country with breakfast in the United States.

Read the following essay written by a student. Underline the thesis statement and the topic sentence in each of the body paragraphs.

Model Essay

Food Customs in Iran

Food customs around the world are strongly connected to culture, tradition, and geography. We can see this in my country, Iran. It has a variable climate, which gives us the advantage of having a large variety of foods to eat. However, what we eat is still influenced by our traditions and geography, as we can see in the similarities and differences between the north and south of Iran.

Many of the food customs are similar everywhere in the country. For example, in both northern and southern Iran, food is eaten with one's hand and a piece of bread instead of using utensils. Rice is an important staple in Iran, and it is a part of almost every meal in both the north and the south. Another similarity between the north and south is eating fish, since both areas are near seas: the Caspian Sea in the north and the Persian Gulf in the south.

Because the north of Iran is quite different from the south, there are several differences in eating habits between the two areas. Northern Iran faces the Caspian Sea where we find the special fish from which the famous caviar is made, which northerners love to eat. Because of the Mediterranean climate in the north, rice is one of the major crops, and it plays an important role at the table in northern Iran. It is served at all ceremonies. As a tradition, northerners conduct a rice ceremony every year by putting rice twigs in the paddy and singing songs. In southern Iran, which faces the Persian Gulf, a variety of seafoods, especially the white fish, make up the favorite dishes. Although rice is important and a part of most meals, the south is better known for its vegetables and fruits. Dates, in particular, are important and are a major export to Western countries.

In conclusion, Iran is a large country with a diverse geography and people. As in all large countries, a variety of customs can be found on all points of the compass. Food customs in particular are influenced by climate and location, making Iran a very interesting country in which to live and eat!

Organizing

Comparing and Contrasting

In this unit, you will learn how to organize a comparison and contrast essay. When we *compare,* we look at the similarities between two things, people, or ideas. When we *contrast,* we look at the differences. It is important to remember these points when comparing and contrasting:

1. The two things that you compare and contrast must be of the same general class. You could not compare and contrast a mouse with an elephant, but you could compare and contrast the African elephant with the Indian elephant.

2. When you compare and contrast two things, the points you use for support must be used for both things. For example, if, in writing about the food of one area, you discuss the vegetables and fruit, the ways of cooking, and the use of spices, you must also discuss these points about the other area.

There are several ways of organizing a comparison and contrast essay. In this chapter, we will look at the most basic pattern, which is called *block organization.*

In block organization, all the similarities are discussed in one block (one or more paragraphs). Then the differences are discussed in another block. The block organization pattern looks like this:

Topic: The Similarities and Differences in the Food of the North and the South of China

I.   Similarities
    A.   Basic ingredients
    B.   Use of spices
    C.   Famous dishes

II. Differences
    A.   Basic ingredients
    B.   Use of spices
    C.   Famous dishes

Comparison and Contrast Words

In order to write a good comparison and contrast essay, it is important to use the correct comparison and contrast words to introduce your points. The following is a list of some of the words and phrases.

Comparison Words and Phrases

Sentence Connectors	Clause Connectors	Others
similarly	as	like (+ noun)
likewise	just as	similar to (+ noun)
also	and	just like (+ noun)
too		(be) similar to
		(be) the same as
		both . . . and
		not only . . . but also

Contrast Words and Phrase

Sentence Connectors	Clause Connectors	Others
however	although	but
nevertheless	even though	yet
in contrast	while	despite (+ noun)
on the other hand	whereas	in spite of (+ noun)
on the contrary		

Using *while* and *whereas*

While and **whereas** have the same meaning and are both used in the same way. Both words are used to show that something is in contrast to or directly the opposite of something else. They can be used at the beginning or in the middle of a sentence.

The meat is sweet, **whereas** the vegetables are salty.
The meat is sweet, **while** the vegetables are salty.
While the vegetables are salty, the meat is sweet.
Whereas the vegetables are salty, the meat is sweet.

While and **whereas** can be used with either of the elements you are comparing with no change in meaning. Note the use of commas with **while** and **whereas.**

Exercise 1

Join the two sentences using **while** or **whereas** at the beginning of the sentence. Use the correct punctuation.

1. In New Mexico, fresh fruit is popular for dessert. In New England, pies are often served.

   _____

   _____

2. In New Mexico, peppers and corn are popular as vegetables. In New England, potatoes and carrots are eaten.

   _____

   _____

3. In New Mexico, chicken and beef appear in many recipes. In New England, fish is popular in many dishes.

   _____

   _____

4. The British put milk in their tea. The Chinese drink it plain.

   _____

   _____

5. The Chinese love to stir-fry and deep-fry. The Vietnamese prefer to steam food or eat it raw.

_____

_____

6. The Chinese and Vietnamese use chopsticks that are about nine inches long and round at the eating end. The Japanese prefer shorter chopsticks that have a pointed end.

_____

_____

Writing Practice

Choose one of the following topics.
1. Compare and contrast the food in two areas or regions of your country.
2. Compare and contrast the way people eat in this country with the way people eat in your country.
3. Compare and contrast the ways one kind of food (e.g., rice, bread) is eaten by different people.

1. **Pre-writing.**

Work with a partner, a group, or alone.
a. Brainstorm the topic. Choose a pre-writing brainstorming technique you prefer. (See page 208.)
b. Brainstorm for similarities and differences.
c. Work on a thesis statement.

2. **Outlining.**

a. Organize your ideas.
Step 1: Write your thesis statement.
Step 2: Choose three good points of comparison and contrast from your brainstorming activity.
Step 3: Remember to put your three points of comparison and contrast in the same order in the body paragraphs.
b. Make a more detailed outline. The essay outline on page 22 will help you.

3. Write a rough draft.

4. Revise your rough draft.

Using the checklist below, check your rough draft or let your partner check it.

Essay Checklist

Essay Organization

Introduction:	_____ Does it include general statements?
	_____ Is there a thesis statement?
Body:	_____ Does it give similarities and then differences, with points in the same order for each thing?
	_____ Are different transitions used to show comparison and contrast?
Conclusion:	_____ Does it summarize main points or state your thesis again in other words?
	_____ Is there a final comment on the topic?

Paragraph Organization

Topic Sentences:	_____ Does each body paragraph have a topic sentence with a controlling idea?
Supporting Sentences:	_____ Is each paragraph about one main idea? Do your sentences support your topic sentence?
	_____ Do you have specific details or examples to support what you have said?

5. Edit your essay.

Work with a partner or a teacher to edit your essay. Correct spelling, punctuation, vocabulary, and grammar. Read your rough draft and try to find errors in the use of connectors.

Example:

Error: <u>Unless</u> beef and chicken are popular in New Mexico,   *conn*
fish is more popular in Massachusetts.
Correct: Whereas beef and chicken are popular in New Mexico, fish is more popular in Massachusetts.

When you find a mistake of this type, you can mark it with the symbol "conn" (connector). Look at page 207 for other symbols to use when editing your work.

6. Write your final copy.

CHAPTER TEN

Tea, Anyone?

Pre-Reading Activity

Discuss these questions.

1. Can you identify which country uses which type of teaware?
2. How many different types of tea can you name?
3. What is the customary way of drinking tea in your country?

Predicting

Answer the questions. Then compare your ideas with those in the reading.

1. What do you know about tea-drinking ceremonies in different parts of the world?
2. How do you think the following words are related to tea drinking?

   whisk   shoes   garlic   sugar   silver

Tea, Anyone?

There is a saying that the British like a nice cup of tea in the morning and a nice cup of tea at night. And at half past seven, their idea of heaven is a nice cup of tea. They like a nice cup of tea with their dinner and a nice cup of tea with their tea, and before they go to bed, there's a lot to be said for a nice cup of tea!

Sometimes it seems that no one likes tea quite as much as the British do. But, in fact, tea is popular in countries around the world, and many different **rituals** and customs for drinking tea have developed over the centuries. In China and Japan, tea was first used as a medicine; it wasn't until many years later that people there drank tea as a **beverage.** Because tea had been considered a sacred remedy, it was always served with much ceremony.

When the Chinese first started drinking tea, they didn't use teapots. Instead, they put tea leaves and hot water into a small bowl with a cover. Drinkers would bring the bowl to their lips and lift the cover very slightly with their forefingers, just enough to drink the liquid but not the leaves. People drank tea in this way **regardless** of the occasion, and it was always offered to guests.

Tea drinking was an important part of Chinese life, but nowhere in the world did people drink tea with more ceremony than in Japan. There, a strict ritual was set down in the fifteenth century by the first great tea master, Shuko. This tea ceremony is still performed today. Guests must wash their hands and faces and remove their shoes before entering the tearoom through a low doorway that forces them to **stoop** and appear **humble.** As the guests kneel or sit cross-legged on mats, the host places a spoonful of powdered tea into a special bowl, adds boiling water, and then stirs it with a bamboo **whisk.** Although in early tea ceremonies everyone drank from the same bowl, it later became the practice for the host to serve the tea in individual bowls. The guests sip the tea slowly and talk until they have finished drinking. Then they are expected to throw back their heads and take the final sip with a loud sound to show how good the tea is. As the ceremony comes to an end, the guests admire the empty serving bowl for its beauty. The host washes the cups, and the ceremony ends. The formal tea ceremony is certainly not **undertaken** every time someone drinks tea in Japan, but the tea is always served with much care and politeness.

The British also like to be formal and **dignified** when they serve tea. While the Japanese serve green tea in small cups without handles, the British favor the black teas of India and Ceylon served in china cups with handles and matching saucers. In Britain, tea is made in a pot, using one teaspoonful of tea leaves for each cup plus one extra teaspoonful for the pot. Boiling water is poured into the pot, and the tea is left for about five minutes before the host pours for the guests. As in Japan, tea drinking is an important part of daily life in England. Many people drink tea several times a day, and they associate it with relaxation and entertainment. Sharing a cup of tea with guests provides an opportunity for conversation and a quiet moment away from the normal **hustle and bustle.**

Many interesting tea customs have developed over the centuries. In India, for example, you might drink tea with a lot of milk, sugar, cinnamon, and cardamom. The Burmese soak tea leaves in oil and garlic and eat this mixture with dried fish. In Thailand, people chew tea leaves seasoned with salt and other spices. In Iran, perfumed tea is a favorite. It is made by leaving flowers or herbs in the tea container for several days. In Morocco, tea is prepared in a brass or silver teapot to which sugar and mint are added. Then the tea is served in small glasses with mint leaves. If guests accept an offer of tea, they are expected to drink at least three glasses.

Regardless of where or how tea is prepared and served, many people consider it to be an important part of their social life. Having a cup of tea provides a reason for getting together and sharing a moment of conversation. Tea may no longer be considered a sacred cure for all illnesses, but it is a remedy for both the body and the spirit in our sometimes **frantic** lives.

Vocabulary

Meaning

What are the meanings of the underlined words? Circle the letter of each correct answer.

1. Many <u>rituals</u> and customs have developed over the centuries.
   a. rules
   b. stories
   c. ceremonies
   d. laws

2. It was many years before tea was taken as a <u>beverage</u>.
   a. drink
   b. medicine
   c. food
   d. remedy

3. Tea was taken in this way <u>regardless of</u> the occasion.
   a. no matter what
   b. because of
   c. depending upon
   d. due to

4. Guests enter through a low doorway that forces them to <u>stoop</u>.
   a. fall
   b. kneel
   c. bend over
   d. lift their heads

5. The low doorway forces them to stoop and appear <u>humble</u>.
   a. not proud
   b. proud
   c. strong
   d. kind

6. The host stirs the tea with a bamboo <u>whisk</u>.
   a. spoon
   b. beater
   c. knife
   d. stick

7. The tea ceremony is not <u>undertaken</u> every time tea is served in Japan.
   a. expected
   b. completed
   c. admired
   d. performed

8. The British also like to be formal and <u>dignified</u>.
   a. important
   c. strict
   b. well-mannered
   d. plain

9. Tea provides a quiet moment away from the <u>hustle and bustle</u>.
   a. problems
   c. children
   b. rush
   d. routine

10. Tea is a remedy for our body and spirit in our sometimes <u>frantic</u> lives.
    a. very unhealthy
    c. hopeless and boring
    b. calm and quiet
    d. extremely busy

Word Building

Complete the sentences with the correct form of the word in capital letters. You may use your dictionary.

1. POPULAR
   a. Tea has not lost its _____ in England.
   b. Green tea is more _____ than black tea in Japan.

2. FORMAL
   a. In Japan, tea is often served with a great deal of _____.
   b. In England, a friendly chat over a cup of tea does not have to be very _____.

3. POLITE
   a. In Japan, it is _____ to drink tea slowly.
   b. Tea is always served with care and _____.

Comprehension

Looking for the Main Ideas

Circle the letter of the correct answer.

1. Tea _____.
   a. is taken in much the same way everywhere
   b. has led to the development of many different customs
   c. was popular as a social drink before being used as a remedy
   d. is popular in every country

2. The tea ceremony in Japan _____.
   a. is formal and complicated
   b. is similar to the British way of serving tea
   c. was borrowed from the Chinese
   d. is practiced whenever the Japanese drink tea

3. Regardless of the country, tea is _____.
   a. an important part of social life
   b. served very formally
   c. always offered to guests
   d. used as a medicine

Looking for Details

Circle T if the sentence is true. Circle F if the sentence is false.

1. Tea was first used as a medicine in China and Japan.   T   F

2. The Chinese drank their tea from bowls with lids.   T   F

3. Drinking tea never became an important part of
   Chinese life.   T   F

4. The Japanese tea ceremony was recently developed.   T   F

5. During the Japanese tea ceremony, guests must appear
   proud.   T   F

6. At the end of the tea ceremony, it is polite to make a
   loud sound to show how good the tea is.   T   F

7. The British drink tea only in the morning and evening.   T   F

8. The British like to serve tea in a very informal way.   T   F

9. In India, you might get cardamom in your tea.   T   F

10. In Morocco, a guest is expected to drink only one glass
    of tea.   T   F

Making Inferences and Drawing Conclusions

The answers to these questions are not directly stated in the reading.
Write complete sentences.

1. Why do you think tea was served with so much ceremony by the
   ancient Chinese and Japanese?

   _____

   _____

2. Why is tea drinking an important part of British daily life?

   _____

   _____

3. Why is tea considered part of the social life in many countries?

   _____

   _____

4. Why is tea considered a remedy for body and spirit?

   _____

   _____

5.   What effect does the tea ceremony have on people's attitudes toward drinking tea?

_____

_____

Discussion

Discuss these questions with your classmates.

1.   What aspects of the tea-drinking ceremony in Japan do you think are beautiful?

2.   Compare the way Americans drink tea or coffee with the way people drink it in your country.

3.   Describe polite table manners in your country as compared with those in the United States.

4.   What is expected of a host or guest in your country?

Organization

Comparing and Contrasting

In the previous chapter, we looked at block organization of a comparison and contrast essay, in which you discuss the similarities in one block and the differences in another. In this chapter, we will look at *point-by-point organization.* With this type of organization, similarities and differences on the same point are discussed together. The point-by-point organization pattern looks like this:

Topic: The Similarities and Differences in the Food of the North and the South of China

I.   Basic Ingredients
    A.   Similarities: North and South
    B.   Differences: North and South

II. Use of Spices
    A.   Similarities: North and South
    B.   Differences: North and South

III. Famous Chinese Dishes
    A.   Similarities: North and South
    B.   Differences: North and South

Compare this organization with the block organization on page 117. In point-by-point organization, the comparison and contrast of the points may be in any order that is appropriate for the topic. You may place the most important point first or last. In both types of organization, you must use comparison and contrast structure words to show whether your points are similar or different.

Using *although*, *even though*, and *though*

Although, **even though**, and **though** all have the same meaning. They introduce an adverbial clause that shows a contrast or an unexpected idea. These clauses are useful when you are comparing and contrasting something.

Examples:

Although the tea was very special, I didn't like the taste.

Even though the tea was very special, I didn't like the taste.

Though the tea was very special, I didn't like the taste.

Note the use of the comma in the above sentences.

Exercise 1

Combine the two sentences into one sentence using **although** or **even though**.

1. The British are tea drinkers. Many people drink coffee.

   _____

   _____

2. In Asia, people drink tea plain. The British prefer tea with milk added.

   _____

   _____

3. Most people make tea from tea leaves. The Burmese eat tea leaves as salad.

   _____

   _____

4. In Asia and Europe, tea is usually made in a ceramic or china teapot. In Morocco, a brass or silver teapot is used.

   _____

   _____

5. Coffee has been regarded as the most popular beverage in the United States. Soft drinks are consumed twice as much.

_____

_____

Writing Practice

Choose one of the following topics.

1. Compare and contrast the way food is served and eaten in the United States with food customs in your country.
2. Compare and contrast behavior expected from a guest or host in your country with that in the United States.
3. Compare the experience of eating in a restaurant in your country with eating in one in the United States.

1. Pre-writing.

Work with a partner, a group, or alone.

a. Brainstorm the topic. Choose a pre-writing brainstorming technique you prefer. (See page 208.)
b. Brainstorm for similarities and differences.
c. Work on a thesis statement.

2. Outlining.

a. Organize your ideas.
   Step 1: Write your thesis statement.
   Step 2: Choose three good points of comparison and contrast from your brainstorming activity.
   Step 3: Remember to order each point with its similarities and differences.
b. Make a more detailed outline. The essay outline on page 22 will help you.

3. Write a rough draft.

4. Revise your rough draft.

Using the checklist below, check your rough draft or let your partner check it.

Essay Checklist

Essay Organization

Introduction:	_____ Does it include general statements?
	_____ Is there a thesis statement?
Body:	_____ Are paragraphs ordered by points, with similarities and differences for each point?
	_____ Are different transitions used to show comparison and contrast?
Conclusion:	_____ Does it summarize main points or state your thesis again in other words?
	_____ Is there a final comment on the topic?

Paragraph Organization

Topic Sentences:	_____ Does each body paragraph have a topic sentence with a controlling idea?
Supporting Sentences:	_____ Is each paragraph about one main idea? Do your sentences support your topic sentence?
	_____ Do you have specific details or examples to support what you have said?

5. Edit your essay.

Work with a partner or a teacher to edit your essay. Correct spelling, punctuation, vocabulary, and grammar. Read your draft and try to find sentence errors that are fragments, or incomplete sentences.

Example:

Error: <u>Whenever they drank tea politely.</u>   frag
Correct: Whenever they drank tea, they were very polite.

When you find a mistake of this type, you can mark it with the symbol "frag" (fragment). Look at page 207 for other symbols to use when editing your work.

6. Write your final copy.

Do you know these food facts?

Work with a partner or alone to see if you can complete the following food facts. Circle the letter of the best answer.

1. There are many varieties of red peppers, which have a very high vitamin C content. In Mexico today, there are _____ varieties.

   a. 54   b. 21   c. 92

2. Coleslaw is a popular American dish. The _____ first introduced this dish to the United States.

   a. British   b. Germans   c. Dutch

3. It is believed that pasta originally came from _____.

   a. Italy   b. China   c. Spain

4. Leavened bread (bread that is not flat) originated in _____.

   a. Egypt   b. France   c. Greece

5. A French sailor named Frazier brought this fruit back from Chile to Europe. This plant, which adapts itself well to different climates, has a red fruit with tiny seeds outside. The fruit has a special sweet smell owing to its 35 different chemicals. This fruit is the _____.

   a. pineapple   b. strawberry   c. raspberry

6. This food originated with the nomadic Turks. It is made by adding bacteria to milk and keeping the mixture warm for several hours. _____ has recently become popular in Europe and the United States.

   a. Cream cheese   b. Sweet butter   c. Yogurt

7. You have to pick a lot of flowers to get a small amount of this spice. As a result, it is the most expensive spice in the world. _____ is used as a sedative in medicine and to give a yellow color to food, especially rice.

   a. Saffron   b. Curry   c. Yellow mustard

Video Activity • Tortillas Today

1. Before watching the video, answer these questions: What do you know about tortillas? What do they look like? What do they taste like? What are they made from?

2. As you watch the video, listen for the answers to the following questions.

   a. About how many tortillas do Americans eat in a year? _____

   b. What were the earliest tortillas made of? _____

   c. What does the word *tortilla* come from? _____

   d. How many dozen tortillas can new high tech factories bake in an hour? _____

   e. What kind of fat is used in tortillas? _____

3. Discuss these questions: Why are tortillas popular? What advantages do they have? How are they similar to other staple foods? How are they different?

Internet Activity

- Work in groups of three. Each person in the group will use the Internet to find out about the Chinese tea ceremony, the Japanese tea ceremony, or the Korean tea ceremony. Discuss what you learned and make a list of the differences among these three types of tea ceremonies.

- Which web sites provided the best information, and who created them?

Language

CHAPTER ELEVEN

Our Changing Language

American Auto Telephonics Company
February 5, 2003

Dear Sir:

Everybody in our company is very impressed with your latest car phone. What businessman (or his wife?) would want to be without one? Please have your salesmen phone us to arrange a presentation.

Sincerely yours,

Mrs. Jane Johnson

Mrs. Jane Johnson
President

1950   old

American Auto Telephonics Company
February 5, 2003

Dear Sales Agent:

Everybody in our company is very impressed with your latest car phone. What business professional (or business professional's spouse) would want to be without one? Please have your salespeople phone us to arrange a presentation.

Sincerely yours,

Mrs. Jane Johnson

Mrs. Jane Johnson
President

2000   new

Pre-Reading Activity

Discuss these questions.

1. What is the difference between the two letters shown?
2. What words did the writer change?
3. Which letter do you think is better? Why?

Predicting

Answer the questions. Then compare your ideas with those in the reading.

1. Why do you think each of the following words is no longer used in English?

   the elderly   actress   chairman   trashman

2. Can you think of any other words that are no longer used in English?

Our Changing Language

Before computers were invented, the words *byte* and *modem* did not exist, and a *mouse* was something that made some people scream and run away. Words are added to language every day, but not only as new things are invented. Changes in society also cause changes in language. For example, today the people of the **former** Soviet Union use words like *free market* and *capitalism.*

Changes in **attitude** also affect language. As people become more sensitive to the rights and needs of individuals, it becomes necessary to change the words we use to describe them. The elderly are now called *senior citizens.* The handicapped are described as *physically challenged.* Many of the words we once used had negative feelings attached to them. New words show an **awareness** in today's society that differences are good and that everyone deserves respect. Even the names of certain jobs have changed so that workers can be proud of what they do. The trashman is now called a *sanitation worker,* a doorman is an *attendant,* and a janitor is a *custodian.*

Many of the words we use to identify people have changed many times in recent years. Sometimes it is difficult to know what is right and what is wrong. Do we call a person of color a *black* or an *African American?* Is it better to say *native Americans* or *American Indians?* And whatever do we do with the Man of the Year? If we don't know what the proper words are, then we must use sensitivity, respect, and even a little imagination.

One important influence on our language in the past decade has been the changing **role** of women in modern society. There was a time when an unmarried woman was called a **spinster.** But that was before women went into space in rockets, worked underground in mines, and became managers of corporations. As women entered more and more areas that were once thought of as men's jobs, it became necessary to change the job titles. For example, a mailman is now a *mail carrier,* a watchman is a *guard,* a lineman is a *line repairer.* And the Man of the Year? Well, she's the *Newsmaker of the Year.*

These new attitudes have also helped men, and some job titles have been changed to include them. Stewardesses are now called *flight attendants*. A laundress is a *laundry worker*, and a maid is a *houseworker*, because men wash floors too!

Sometimes new words may seem **awkward** and silly, such as *chair* for chairman, *fisher* for fisherman, and *drafter* for draftsman. But change is never easy. People often fight change until it becomes a familiar part of everyday life.

Women have fought long and hard to be treated equally in language as well as in society, because they know that changes in language can cause changes in attitudes. If every person isn't **referred to** as *he*, people will begin to realize that men aren't the only ones who are important or who have made great **achievements**. Most words that indicate only one **gender** have been replaced with words that refer to both males and females. Thus, a poetess is called a *poet*, a waitress is a *server*, and mankind has become *humankind*.

Vocabulary

Meaning

What are the meanings of the underlined words? Circle the letter of each correct answer.

1. The people of the <u>former</u> Soviet Union use words like *capitalism*.
   - a. new
   - b. changing
   - c. traditional
   - d. previous

2. Changes in <u>attitude</u> also affect language.
   - a. the way we feel and think
   - b. the way we move
   - c. the way we speak
   - d. the way we behave

3. New words show an <u>awareness</u> in today's society that differences are good.
   - a. quickness
   - b. confusion
   - c. understanding
   - d. fashion

4. One important influence on our language has been the changing <u>role</u> of women in modern society.
   a. group   c. looks
   b. position   d. occupation

5. Sometimes the new words may seem <u>awkward</u> and silly.
   a. strange   c. incorrect
   b. useless   d. clumsy

6. If every person isn't <u>referred to</u> as *he*, people will realize men aren't the only ones who are important.
   a. talked about   c. thought of
   b. classified   d. treated

7. Men aren't the only ones who are responsible for <u>achievements</u>.
   a. inventions   c. successes
   b. businesses   d. events

8. Most words that indicate only one <u>gender</u> have been replaced with words that refer to both males and females.
   a. group   c. sex
   b. word   d. meaning

Word Building

Complete the sentences with the correct form of the word in capital letters. You may use your dictionary.

1. SENSITIVE
   a. We have to use _____ when describing other people.
   b. We should be _____ to other people's feelings.

2. RESPECT
   a. We can show _____ for a person by using the correct job description.
   b. It is not _____ to use the term *spinster* for an unmarried woman.

3. AWARE
   a. New words show an _____ of changes in society.
   b. Sometimes we are not _____ of how words can influence our attitudes.

Comprehension

Looking for the Main Ideas

Circle the letter of the correct answer.

1. Words are added to language _____.
   a. only when new things are invented
   b. only when society changes
   c. when old words disappear
   d. all the time

2. Language is also affected by _____.
   a. changes in attitude
   b. the actions of individuals
   c. changes in population
   d. the invention of new words

3. An important influence on our language recently has been _____.
   a. the changing role of managers
   b. the changing jobs of men
   c. the changing role of women
   d. the changing role of language

Looking for Details

Scan the reading quickly to find the answers to these questions. Write complete answers.

1. What are the new names for trashman and doorman?

   _____

2. What was an unmarried woman called in the past?

   _____

3. What are today's job titles for a mailman and a watchman?

   _____

4. What do we say instead of Man of the Year?

   _____

5. Women used to be stewardesses, laundresses, and maids. What are these job titles today?

   _____

6. Which three new words may seem awkward?

   _____

7. What do we say instead of *mankind*?

   _____

Making Inferences and Drawing Conclusions

The answers to these questions are not directly stated in the reading. Write complete sentences.

1. Who do you think will fight some of these changes in language?

   _____

   _____

2. Are the new words more or less accurate?

   _____

   _____

3. Why do words for describing people change frequently?

   _____

   _____

4. How have changes in job titles helped both men and women?

   _____

   _____

Discussion

Discuss these questions with your classmates.

1. What do you think of the following new ways to identify people and things? Are these good changes? Can you improve on them? What other words can you think of that could be changed?

Old	New
businessmen	businesspeople
salesman, saleswoman	sales clerk *sales assistant*
deliveryman	deliverer, delivery clerk
manpower	personnel, staff, people power
repairman	repairer
hostess	host
housewife	homemaker
motherland, fatherland	homeland
manmade	synthetic

postman   *post carrier*

2. Describe some changes in the language of your country.
3. Does language change slowly or quickly?
4. What are some causes of language change?

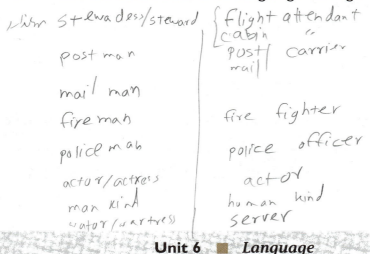

stewardess/steward   *{flight attendant*
                     cabin "
postman   *post/ carrier*
            mail/
mailman
fireman   *fire fighter*
policeman   *police officer*
actor/actress   *actor*
mankind   *humankind*
waiter/waitress   *server*

chairman   *chairperson*
sportsman/—   *sportsperson*   *athletic*

WRITING

Read the following essay written by a student. Underline the thesis statement and the topic sentence in each of the body paragraphs.

Model Essay

Learning English Is Important to Me

When I first came to the United States of America, I found out the importance of knowing English. Whenever I went to the market to buy food, to the post office to mail a letter, or to take a bus to the bank, I had to communicate in English or things would not go smoothly. But the two most important reasons for learning English for me are to be able to go through the interview process to get a job and to be able to read English to know what is going on in the world.

First, learning English is essential if I wish to go through the interview process to get a job. It is important to feel comfortable with the language and be able to converse without hesitation with the interviewer. Even if the interview may be in another language, sometimes the interviewer will switch to English just to test your fluency. But conversation is not enough; I must be able to understand formal written English, including contracts. When I was in Hong Kong, I went for an interview and was given a letter of employment to read and sign. The letter stated, "You will have a nine-month probation period, and one month's notice or payment in lieu of notice has to be given if either party wants to terminate the contract during the probation period." I did not know what "payment in lieu of" or "terminate" meant. I could not ask the interviewer or I would not get the job. I signed the contract and started the job. I quit six months later without prior notice. Because I did not understand the contract, I lost a month's salary.

Second, learning English is important for me because I want to know what is going on around me in the world. When I read newspapers and magazines in my own language, I feel I am not getting enough news of the world. I believe that Western reporters communicate all kinds of news in greater detail, and this will give me a different perspective. Also, being able to read magazines and newspapers in English will keep me abreast of the technological changes that will be affecting us all. With recent advances in technology, the world is changing rapidly in many fields, such as business, arts, and medicine. These changes will affect me soon, and it is important for me to read and keep up with these changes.

In conclusion, it is important for me to learn English so that I will feel confident about myself when I go for a job interview again. It is also important because I want to know what is happening in the world around me, and by learning English I can do this. In fact, learning English is the answer to a lot of the things that I need and want.

Organizing

Cause and Effect

In this unit, you will look at a situation *(effect)* and examine the reasons *(causes)* for it. Usually there is more than one reason for a situation. It is important to look at all the reasons. When there are many reasons, there is usually one that is most important.

When you write about the causes of an effect, remember the following.

1. Look at all the possible causes and discuss them.
2. Support all the causes. Give good examples.
3. State your most important cause last. This will make your essay more interesting. If you state your most important cause first, the reader will not have anything to look forward to.

Look at the model student essay. Notice these points.

- The thesis statement tells the reader what the situation is and that there are reasons, or causes, for this situation.
- Each of the body paragraphs gives a cause or reason and supports it with examples.
- Each paragraph starts with a different transition. The transitions used for chronological order can also be used to introduce a cause.

Transitions for Showing Cause: *because* and *as*

Because and **as** introduce a reason clause. They both answer the question "Why?" Both **because** and **as** can be used at the beginning of a sentence or in the middle.

Example:

Statement: Language is changing.
Reason: The roles of women are changing in modern society.

Language is changing $\begin{Bmatrix} \textbf{as} \\ \textbf{because} \end{Bmatrix}$ the roles of women are changing in modern society.

or

$\begin{Bmatrix} \textbf{Because} \\ \textbf{As} \end{Bmatrix}$ the roles of women are changing in modern society, language is changing.

Note: Use a comma after the reason if you start the sentence with **because** or **as.**

Join the sentences with **as.** Write each sentence in two ways—with **as** in the middle and with **as** at the beginning.

1. Language changes. Society changes.

    language changes as ~~the~~ society changes

    a As ~~the~~ society change , languag chaiys

2. Words are added to the language every day. New things are invented.

    As New thigs are invented , word

    words areadd   as new thing are invented

3. There is a need to change some job titles. Women are entering areas that were once thought of as men's jobs.

    As Woman are   , there is

    There is a ncch   as wu

Writing Practice

Choose one of the following topics.

1. As society and times change, words in English (or your language) need to change, too. Give two or more reasons for this.
2. The spelling of English words needs to change. Give two or more reasons for this.
3. Learning English is important in my life. Give two or more reasons for this.

1. Pre-writing.

    Work with a partner, a group, or alone.

    a. Brainstorm the topic. Choose a pre-writing brainstorming technique you prefer. (See page 208.)
    b. Brainstorm for reasons and ideas about each reason.
    c. Work on a thesis statement.

2. Outlining.

    a. Organize your ideas.

        Step 1: Write your thesis statement.

        Step 2: Pick the two best reasons from your brainstorming activity (or choose three reasons for a three-paragraph body).

        Step 3: Remember to begin your paragraphs with different transition words for showing causes and their order of importance. Keep your most important cause for last.

    b. Make a more detailed outline. The essay outline below will help you.

Cause and Effect Essay Outline

Introduction	*Thesis:* situation and reasons for it
Body	*Topic Sentence:* first cause or reason Supporting sentences
	Topic Sentence: second cause or reason Supporting sentences
Conclusion	Restatement of thesis Final comment

---

3. Write a rough draft.

4. Revise your rough draft.

    Using the checklist below, check your rough draft or let your partner check it.

Essay Checklist
Essay Organization

Introduction:
- ＿＿＿ Does it include general statements?
- ＿＿＿ Is there a thesis statement?

Body:
- ＿＿＿ Are reasons organized logically, with the most important reason last?
- ＿＿＿ Are different transitions used to show cause and order?

Conclusion:	____ Does it summarize main points or state your thesis again in other words?
	____ Is there a final comment on the topic?

Paragraph Organization

Topic Sentence:	____ Does each body paragraph have a topic sentence with a controlling idea?
Supporting Sentences:	____ Is each paragraph about one main idea? Do your sentences support your topic sentence?
	____ Do you have specific factual details to support what you have said?

5. **Edit your essay.**

Work with a partner or a teacher to edit your essay. Correct spelling, punctuation, vocabulary, and grammar. Read your rough draft and try to find errors in the use of pronoun reference.

Example:

Error: A retired person may feel better about <u>his</u> age   pro re
if <u>he</u> is called a senior citizen.

Correct (version 1): A retired person may feel better about his or her age if he or she is called a senior citizen.

Correct (version 2): Retired people may feel better about their age if they are called senior citizens.

When you find a mistake of this type, you can mark it with the symbol "pro re" (pronoun reference). Look at page 207 for other symbols to use when editing your work.

6. **Write your final copy.**

CHAPTER TWELVE

English Around the World

Pre-Reading Activity

Discuss these questions.

1. Describe the picture. What country do you think it is?

2. In your country, what English words do you see on the streets, in shops, and in eating places?

3. Why do people like to use these English words?

Predicting

Answer the questions. Then compare your ideas with those in the reading.

1. These words are all taken from English and used in other languages. What do you think the original English words are?

   rushawa   sueter   herkot   te le fung

2. Why do you think other languages borrow words from English?

English Around the World

Do you speak English? That question is frequently asked in countries around the world. Although there are almost 3,000 languages, English is the most universal. It is the official language in over 40 countries and the most used language in international business, science, and medicine.

Even in countries where English is not the first language, a number of English words are used. No other language is **borrowed** from more often than English. For example, a French worker looks forward to *le weekend.* A Romanian shopper catches a ride on the *trolleybus.* A Chinese businessperson talks on the *te le fung* (telephone). Some Swedish schoolgirls have even started making the plural forms of words by adding *-s,* as in English, instead of the Swedish way of adding *-ar, -or,* or *-er.*

Hundreds of words borrowed from English can now be found in other languages, words such as *soda, hotel, golf, tennis, jeans, O.K., baseball,* and *airport.* Although many words are used just as they are, others are changed to make them more like the native language and therefore easier to say and remember. Thus, a Japanese worker gets stuck in *rushawa* (rush-hour) traffic. A Spanish mother tells her child to put on her *sueter* (sweater), and a Ukrainian man goes to the barber for a *herkot* (haircut).

English is everywhere. It is on signs, clothing, soft drinks, and household products around the world. In spite of the popularity of English words and phrases, however, they are not always welcome. Some people think that the use of English words is **threatening** the purity of their native language. In 1975, the French started a commission to try to stop, and even give **fines** for, the use of English words. Some countries have tried to **eliminate** English as their official language in order to save their native tongue.

On the other hand, some people believe that English should be the international language. They give a number of reasons for this, such as the cost of translations and the misunderstandings that result from language differences. They believe that things would run more smoothly if everyone spoke the same language.

"What would become of our many different cultures?" others argue. "Certainly the world would be a much less interesting place," they add. Indeed, there is serious **concern** on the part of language experts that many languages are disappearing. In some parts of the world, only a few people are left who can speak the native tongue. In Ireland, for example, there are only a few small areas where people speak Gaelic, the native Irish language. One expert says that half of the world's languages are dying because children are no longer learning them.

Languages have changed and disappeared throughout history. With progress, change is **inevitable.** Some things are worth **preserving.** Others are not. The difficulty is in deciding what is worth keeping. Because people have very strong feelings about the importance of their native language, we probably will not have a universal language in the near future. What is certain, however, is that English words will continue to **pop up** everywhere, from Taiwan to Timbuktu, whether some people like it or not.

Vocabulary

Meaning

What are the meanings of the underlined words? Circle the letter of each correct answer.

1. No other language is <u>borrowed</u> from more than English.
   a. born
   b. taken
   c. developed
   d. copied

2. The purity of their native language is <u>threatened</u>.
   a. improved
   b. in doubt
   c. prevented
   d. in danger

3. The French gave <u>fines</u> for the use of English.
   a. punishment in the form of taking money
   b. points
   c. prison punishment
   d. rewards

4. Some countries have tried to <u>eliminate</u> English as their official language as a way of saving their native tongue.
   a. remove
   b. welcome
   c. exchange
   d. provide

5. There is serious <u>concern</u> that many languages are disappearing.
   a. hope
   b. worry
   c. discussion
   d. problem

6. With progress, change is <u>inevitable</u>.
   a. impossible to stop
   b. possible
   c. not possible
   d. avoidable

7. Some things are worth <u>preserving</u>.
   a. changing
   b. avoiding
   c. continuing
   d. keeping

8. It is certain that English words will continue to <u>pop up</u> everywhere.
   a. appear
   b. die
   c. change
   d. develop

Word Building

Complete the sentences with the correct form of the word in capital letters. You may use your dictionary.

1. UNDERSTAND
   a. It is _____ that some people dislike foreign words in their language.
   b. I _____ the instructions because they used many words that I knew from English.

2. SPEAK
   a. English is _____ in many countries around the world.
   b. _____ English can help you in business, science, and medicine.

3. THREAT
   a. Some people feel that English is a _____ to their own native language.
   b. Others feel that English does not _____ other languages, but can be an international language.

Comprehension

Looking for the Main Ideas

Circle the letter of the best answer.

1. No other language _____.
   a. has more letters than English
   b. has as many foreign words as English
   c. is official in every country, as English is
   d. lends so many words to other languages

2. English words _____.
   a. are changed by other languages
   b. replace words in other languages
   c. make other languages less comprehensible
   d. are welcomed by other languages

3. In the near future, English _____.
   a. will disappear completely
   b. will continue to appear in other languages
   c. will be the only language in the world
   d. will have to change

Looking for Details

Scan the reading quickly to find the answers to these questions. Write complete answers.

1. In how many countries is English the official language?

   _____

   _____

2. What has the Swedish language borrowed from English?

   _____

   _____

3. Give examples of two English words that have been changed to make them more like the native language of the speakers.

   _____

   _____

4. What did the French do in 1975 to stop the use of English words?

   _____

   _____

5. What is Gaelic?

   _____

   _____

6. Who is saying that many of the world's languages are disappearing?

   _____

   _____

Making Inferences and Drawing Conclusions

The answers to these questions are not directly stated in the reading. Write complete sentences.

1. Which country feels that the purity of its language is threatened by having English words added to it?

   _____

   _____

2. What is the main language spoken in Ireland?

   _____

   _____

3. What do you think will happen to Gaelic in Ireland?

   _____

   _____

4. Which languages do you think are disappearing?

   _____

   _____

5. What are the benefits of borrowing words from English? What are the drawbacks?

   _____

   _____

Discussion

Discuss these questions with your classmates.

1. Make a list of ten of the most popular English words in your country, and write how you say them. Compare your list with that of a classmate.
2. Why do you think English has become a global language?
3. Why have languages disappeared throughout history? Give some examples.
4. How would you stop a language from dying out?

Organizing

Cause and Effect Essay

In Chapter 10, we looked at an essay where you give reasons for something. In this chapter, we will look at how to organize an essay that gives reasons for something and then discusses the results. This is a *cause and effect* essay.

There are two ways to organize a cause and effect essay: block organization and chain organization.

1. *Block Organization:* You discuss all of the causes in one block (one, two, or three paragraphs, depending on the number of causes). Then you discuss all the effects in another block.

Causes
Effects

2. *Chain Organization:* You discuss a first cause and then its effect, a second cause and its effect, a third cause and its effect, and so on.

Cause ↓ Effect
Cause ↓ Effect

The type of organization you choose for your cause and effect essay will depend on your topic. Some topics work better when organized in a block, while others work better when organized in a chain. If the causes and effects are closely related, it is better to use a chain organization.

Which Are the Causes and Which Are the Effects?

It is important to understand the difference between the cause and the effect. Remember that an effect can have several causes.

Examples:

Today the Japanese use many English words. *(effect)*
The Japanese watch American TV programs. *(cause)*
The Japanese listen to American pop music. *(cause)*

Identify which is the cause and which is the effect.

_____ 1.   Half of the world's languages are dying.
_____   Children no longer learn them.

_____ 2.   The Umutina tribal language of South America disappeared.
_____   The only person who spoke the language died in 1988.

_____ 3.   Children in France are not learning the Breton language in
           schools.
_____   The Breton language in France is near extinction.

_____ 4.   The Amish, a religious group in America, have kept their
           language, Pennsylvania Dutch, alive for three centuries.
_____   They speak Pennsylvania Dutch at home.
_____   They do not have telephones or television.

Cause and Effect Structure Words

Certain words and phrases signal a cause or an effect. Here are some
that you may already know.

Cause Structure Words	Effect Structure Words
The first reason . . .	The first effect . . .
The next cause . . .	As a result, . . .
Because . . .	Consequently, . . .

The cause structure words signal a reason for something.

Example:

Because children are no longer learning the native tongues of their
grandfathers, . . .

The effect structure words signal the result.

Example:

Consequently, many languages are disappearing.

Using *therefore* and *consequently*

Therefore and **consequently** are sentence connectors. They connect two clauses when the second clause is the result of the first clause. **Consequently** and **therefore** have the same meaning as the coordinator **so**.

Example:

English is the most universal language. *(statement)*
It is the language most used for science, medicine, and business. *(result)*

English is the most universal language; $\left\{ \begin{array}{c} \textbf{consequently} \\ \textbf{therefore} \end{array} \right\}$, it is the language most used for science, medicine, and business.

Note: Use a semicolon before and a comma after **consequently** and **therefore.**

Exercise 2

Read the pairs of sentences. Choose the clause that gives the result. Then combine the sentences, adding **therefore** or **consequently** before the result clause. Punctuate the sentences.

1. Sometimes English words are changed to make them more like the native language. They are easier to say and remember.

   _____

   _____

2. In France, where English is not spoken, many words are borrowed. A French worker looks forward to *le weekend.*

   _____

   _____

3. English words are becoming popular in other languages. Some people are afraid that the purity of their language is threatened.

   _____

   _____

4. There will be no universal language in the near future. People have strong feelings about the importance of their language.

   _____

   _____

Writing Practice

Choose one of the following topics.

1. The causes and effects of having English as a global language.
2. The effects English (American music, food, sports, etc.) has had on your language and culture.
3. The effects the English language and culture have had on you.

1. **Pre-writing.**

   Work with a partner, a group, or alone.

   a. Brainstorm the topic. Divide your paper into two columns. List the causes on one side and the effects on the other.

   b. Brainstorm for ideas for each cause and effect. Choose a pre-writing brainstorming technique that you prefer. (See page 208.)

   c. Work on a thesis statement.

2. **Outlining.**

   a. Organize your ideas.

   Step 1: Write your thesis statement.

   Step 2: Pick the two best causes and effects from your brainstorming activity.

   Step 3: Remember to use a variety of cause and effect structure words and connectors.

   b. Make a more detailed outline. The essay outline below will help you.

Cause and Effect Essay Outline

Introduction	*Thesis:* situation and reasons for it
Body	*Topic Sentence:* first cause or reason Supporting sentences
	Topic Sentence: second cause or reason Supporting sentences
Conclusion	Restatement of thesis Final comment

3. Write a rough draft.

4. Revise your rough draft.

Using the checklist below, check your rough draft or let your partner check it.

Essay Checklist

Essay Organization

Introduction: ____ Does it include general statements?
            ____ Is there a thesis statement?

Body: ____ Are causes and effects logically organized?
            ____ Are cause and effect structure words used?

Conclusion: ____ Does it summarize main points or state your thesis again in other words?
            ____ Is there a final comment on the topic?

Paragraph Organization

Topic Sentence: ____ Does each body paragraph have a topic sentence with a controlling idea?

Supporting Sentences: ____ Is each paragraph about one main idea? Do your sentences support your topic sentence?
            ____ Do you have specific details to support what you have said?

5. Edit your essay.

Work with a partner or a teacher to edit your essay. Correct spelling, punctuation, vocabulary, and grammar. Read your draft and try to find errors in word order.

Example:

Error: Society changes slowly, and so <u>language does.</u>   *wo*
Correct: Society changes slowly, and so does language.

When you find a mistake of this type, you can mark it with the symbol "wo" (word order). Look at page 207 for other symbols to use when editing your work.

6. Write your final copy.

Do you know these facts about language?

Work with a partner or alone to see if you can answer these questions.

1. How many words (not including technical terms) does the English language contain?

    a. 300,000   b. 490,000   c. 600,000

2. English is full of words borrowed from other languages. Which languages do you think these words came from?

    boss   karate   robot

    disco   shampoo   ketchup

    a. Chinese _____

    b. French _____

    c. Dutch _____

    d. Japanese _____

    e. Czech _____

    f. Indian _____

    Do you know any other borrowed words?

3. Which language is spoken by the greatest number of people in the world?

    a. Spanish   b. Chinese   c. English

4. How many alphabets are used in the world?

    a. 10   b. 26   c. 65

5. What is Ameslan?

    a. a language spoken by the Dutch

    b. a language spoken in Papua New Guinea

    c. American Sign Language

Video Report • Computer Faces :-)

1. Have you ever used a computer smiley face in an email message? Do you think such symbols help people communicate? Why?

2. Review these terms before you watch the video: *jest* (noun), *ironic* (adjective), *phenomenon* (noun), *frown* (noun or verb).

3. As you watch the video, listen for the answers to these questions. Put a check before the correct answers.

   a. About how many years before the video did smiley faces come into use?

   ____ five   ____ fifteen
   ____ ten   ____ twenty

   b. What kind of face follows the statement: "My pay has just been cut"?

   ____ frowning   ____ silly
   ____ smiley   ____ threatening

   c. About how many smileys has David Sanderson collected?

   ____ 700   ____ 1,000
   ____ 900   ____ 2,000

   d. Smiley faces are useful because . . .

   ____ they add humor   ____ they are literary
   ____ they add expression   ____ they are unusual

4. Why do so many people like to use smileys? Do good writers have to use smileys? Why or why not? Do you think they are here to stay?

Internet Activity

- Look up "gender and language" on the Internet to find out about recent ideas on the use of gender-specific words in the English language. Find three examples of possible problems and suggestions for how to solve them.

- How can the Internet help you learn about language and about writing skills? What did you learn from doing this activity?

Environment

CHAPTER THIRTEEN

Zoos

Pre-Reading Activity

Discuss these questions.

1. What zoos do you know of, and how are the animals kept in them?
2. Why do we keep animals in zoos?
3. Are animals happy in zoos?

Predicting

Answer the questions. Then compare your ideas with those in the reading.

1. What are the reasons for keeping animals in zoos? Make a list.
2. How is each of the following words connected with the topic of zoos?

confine	conserve	observe	capture
educate	breed	control	

Zoos

It was in 1826 that the Zoological Society **was founded** in London. In 1867, the title was shortened to *zoo*. Later on, in 1892, the Englishman Henry Salt, in his book *Animal Rights,* was one of the first to protest against keeping animals in cages. He did not like the idea because of the way the animals were **confined** and also the way animals in zoos "lose their character." Since then, many people have criticized zoos for these reasons. However, zoos claim that their role is to educate the public and **conserve** animals. These aims are not bad in themselves. It is the way in which they are carried out that we must consider.

Zoos claim that they have an important educational function. Is this true? In reality, most people go to zoos for entertainment. This is what sells the tickets and pays the bills. Zoos say they give people the opportunity to see the wonders of nature and its wild animals. In fact, they are showing us animals that have lost their **dignity:** animals with sad and empty eyes. The conditions under which animals are kept in zoos changes their behavior. Animals, like humans, are affected by their environment. After months and years in a cage without any interest, animals begin to lose their natural characteristics. Many animals in zoos get signs of "zoochosis," abnormal behavior which includes endlessly **pacing up and down** and rocking from side to side. It is caused by lack of space, lack of interest, lack of company, and an unsuitable diet. Two polar bears in Bristol Zoo in England have been confined in a small area for 28 years and show all the signs of zoochosis. How can people observe wild animals under such conditions and believe that they are being educated? To learn about wild animals one must observe them in the wild where they live.

Zoos also claim that they are conserving **endangered species** in the hope of returning them to the wild in the future. Out of about 10,000 zoos that exist around the world, only about 500 register their animals with an international species **database,** and only about five or ten percent of these actually work with endangered species. Zoos have projects where they breed animals in zoos for the purpose of conservation. However, most animals do not need help in breeding;

they have been doing it for a long time without any help. Animals have been endangered because their natural surroundings have been destroyed by humans. It is true that zoos have had several success stories with zoo-bred animals. One was the golden lion tamarin, a species of monkey, which had almost become **extinct** because humans destroyed its natural habitat and too many were captured for pets and zoos. Over 100 tamarins were bred in zoos, and when they were released into the wild, only 30 survived. Some were unable to live life in the wild—they were not able to climb trees, or when they did, they fell off; some did not even move; some were not used to a natural diet. It is a risky business to re-introduce zoo-bred animals to the wild, because if they have lost their **instinct** for survival and cannot **adapt** quickly enough, they will die.

In conclusion, it seems that zoos are trying to fulfill their goals to educate and conserve but in the process are harming the animals themselves. What is the solution then? One solution is to protect the natural homes or habitats of animals. Another possibility is to have habitat preserves where wild animals live with the least possible human interference. If the money and expertise that zoos are using today were redirected to habitat preservation and management, we would not have the problems of having to conserve species whose natural homes have disappeared. Nonetheless, there also has to be an international effort to control pollution and the illegal capturing of endangered species.

Vocabulary

Meaning

Complete each definition with one of the following words.

was founded	dignity	adapt
confined	pacing up and down	instinct
database	an endangered species	
conserve	extinct	

1. When you are walking back and forth as if worried, you are

   _____ .

2. When animals or humans do things naturally, without learning, they do it by _____ .

3. When there are so few examples of a kind of animal or plant that it might die out completely, it is _____.

4. An animal or plant that no longer exists is _____.

5. A person or animal that has _____ has self-respect and a nobleness of character.

6. The year an organization such as the London Zoological Society was started or established is the date it _____.

7. To save is to _____.

8. Some zoos have a _____ with lists of endangered animals.

9. Something or someone in a cage or prison is _____.

10. To change so as to be able to live or work in new conditions is to _____.

Word Building

Complete the sentences with the correct form of the word in capital letters. You may use your dictionary.

1. RISK
   a. One _____ of keeping animals in zoos is that they will die of boredom.
   b. It is a _____ business to keep wild animals in small confined spaces.

2. ENTERTAIN
   a. Some people go to zoos for _____.
   b. Children find it _____ to watch the penguins.

3. SURVIVE
   a. Some animals cannot _____ in zoos.
   b. Zoos can help protect the _____ of certain species.

Comprehension

Looking for the Main Ideas

Circle the letter of the correct answer.

1. People have criticized zoos for confining animals and making them "lose their character" since _____.
    a.   1867
    b.   Henry Salt wrote his book *Animal Rights*
    c.   zoos were founded
    d.   zoochosis appeared

2. Animals kept in zoos _____.
    a.   may suffer from zoochosis
    b.   have dignity
    c.   are good for the environment
    d.   are for conservation only

3. There are programs to conserve endangered species _____.
    a.   in every zoo   c.   in some zoos
    b.   only in the wild   d.   in most zoos

Looking for Details

Complete the following sentences.

1. The Zoological Society started in the city of _____.

2. The term *zoo* was short for _____.

3. Henry Salt protested against keeping animals in cages in his book _____.

4. Zoochosis is caused by _____, _____, and _____.

5. Signs of zoochosis include _____ and _____.

6. In Bristol Zoo in England, two polar bears have zoochosis because

   _____ .

7. There are about _____ zoos around the world.

8. The golden lion tamarin almost became extinct because humans captured the tamarins for _____ and _____ .

9. When 100 zoo-bred tamarins were put into the wild, only

   _____ .

10. Some tamarins could not climb trees or fell off them. Some _____ ; some were not used to different food.

Making Inferences and Drawing Conclusions

The answers to these questions are not directly stated in the reading. Write complete sentences.

1. What did Salt mean by writing that animals in zoos "lose their character"?

   _____

   _____

2. What is meant by animals that "have lost their dignity"?

   _____

   _____

3. What kinds of natural characteristics can animals lose in a zoo?

   _____

   _____

4. How can we protect the natural homes or habitats of animals?

   _____

   _____

5. How do concerns about zoos reflect changing attitudes in society?

_____

_____

Discussion

Discuss these questions with your classmates.

1. Are zoos necessary? What additional arguments can you find in favor of zoos?
2. If we keep zoos, how do you think animals should be kept in them?
3. Do you think zoos are educational? Explain why or why not.
4. When you visit a zoo, do you go for education or entertainment?

Read the following essay written by a student. Underline the thesis statement and the topic sentence in each of the body paragraphs.

Model Essay

Argument for Zoos

In the past, zoos were places where we saw single animals in small, empty cages. Today zoos are changing in design; animals have more space, and some live in groups. Many zoos try to put animals in an environment that is similar to where they live in the wild. Some people who believe in animal rights argue against having zoos, because they think it is wrong to put animals in cages. I support the idea of having zoos, because they allow us to see wild animals that we cannot see otherwise, and they help endangered species from becoming extinct.

The first reason for having zoos is that they allow people to see wild animals that they could not see otherwise. Zoos are the only places for most people who live in cities to see wild animals. Seeing wild animals on nature documentary programs or in books is not the same thing as seeing animals in real life. Zoos educate people about wild animals and teach them to understand and care about them. That is why there are school trips to the zoo, where the zookeepers tell students about the animals.

Secondly, many endangered species would become extinct if we did not have zoos. Zoos have saved numerous species from dying out or have helped animals get healthier and returned them back to the wild. For example, San Diego Zoo in California has special programs to save the giant pandas and white rhinoceroses. There is also a great deal of research that goes on in many zoos to study animal behavior.

In conclusion, zoos have a valuable role to play: they have an educational role and help to preserve certain species. It is important for animals to be treated well and kept in an environment which is as natural as possible. Many zoos today are responding to their critics and changing the way they keep animals so that they can continue their role without harming animals.

Organizing

Writing an Argument Essay

When you write an argument or persuasion essay, you give reasons to support your ideas for or against something. When writing your essay, you may use description, comparison and contrast, or cause and effect to illustrate your points.

First, find relevant reasons to support your argument. Your reasons may be facts or opinions. Then develop your reasons into paragraphs, using relevant facts, examples, and opinions. You may use the following transitions to begin your body paragraphs:

The first reason . . .
The second reason . . .
In addition, . . .

When you list the points to support your argument, some may be facts and some may be opinions. *Facts* are statements that are known to be true. *Opinions* are personal beliefs that may or may not be true. You may use both facts and opinions in your argument essay. However, if you use only opinions, your argument may not be so convincing. It is, therefore, important to distinguish between fact and opinion.

Example:

Fact: In four months, thirty animals died at Taronga Zoo in Sydney, Australia.
Opinion: Animals get sick and die in zoos.

Which of the following statements are facts and which are opinions? Write F for fact and O for opinion.

_____ 1. A study at a U.S. zoo found most visitors spend less than three minutes looking at each exhibit and some as little as eight seconds.

_____ 2. Zoo life is easier than life in the wild.

_____ 3. Success stories of zoo-bred animals include the Arabian oryx, the Round Island boa, and the Mauritian pink pigeon.

_____ 4. It is estimated that every day between 50 and 100 species of plant or animal become extinct.

_____ 5. Zoos give pleasure to people.

_____ 6. A lot has been learned by studying animals in captivity.

_____ 7. Zoos in the United States are covered under the federal Animal Welfare Act, which sets housing and maintenance standards for captive animals.

_____ 8. Zoos encourage sympathy and interest in wild animals.

Relevant or Not Relevant

It is important that the statements in support of your argument be relevant. In other words, they should be directly connected to the argument.

Work in groups or alone to decide which of the following statements are relevant to the argument given below. Write R for relevant and NR for not relevant.

Argument: Ecotourism is the new force in the preservation of animals.

_____ 1.   It works in cooperation with the people of the surrounding area, and alternative jobs are given to hunters.

_____ 2.   The best guides are often ex-hunters who discourage others from illegal hunting.

_____ 3.   People will be able to watch wildlife in their natural habitats.

_____ 4.   Nature-based tourism has been practiced for decades in national parks and other protected areas without any problems.

_____ 5.   High levels of ecotourism will not be compatible with the environment.

_____ 6.   For reasons of age, health, or money, many people will not be able to go on these trips.

After giving reasons with relevant and specific details to support your argument, you can conclude with one of the following:

In conclusion, . . .
Finally, . . .
Thus, . . .
For these reasons, . . .
As a result, . . .

Writing Practice

Choose one of the following topics.

1. Write an argument in favor of or against using animals in circuses.
2. Write an argument in favor of or against keeping pets.
3. Write an argument in favor of or against hunting animals for entertainment.
4. Write an argument in favor of or against horse racing or greyhound racing.

1. **Pre-writing.**

    Work with a partner, a group, or alone.

    a. Brainstorm the topic. Choose a pre-writing brainstorming technique you prefer. (See page 208.)
    b. Brainstorm for reasons either for or against the argument. Brainstorm for possible supporting details for each reason.
    c. Work on a thesis statement.

2. **Outlining.**

    a. Organize your ideas.
        Step 1: Write your thesis statement.
        Step 2: Pick the two best reasons in favor of or against the argument from your brainstorming activity.
        Step 3: Remember to begin your paragraphs with different transition words for giving reasons.
    b. Make a more detailed outline. The essay outline on page 22 will help you.

3. **Write a rough draft.**

4. **Revise your rough draft.**

    Using the checklist below, check your rough draft or let your partner check it.

    ### Essay Checklist

    Essay Organization

Introduction:	_____ Does it include general statements?
	_____ Is there a thesis statement?
Body:	_____ Do you give relevant reasons for your argument, with a paragraph for each reason? Are your reasons identified as opinion or fact?
	_____ Are different transitions used to show reasons and order?
Conclusion:	_____ Does it summarize main points or state your thesis again in other words?
	_____ Is there a final comment on the topic?

    Paragraph Organization

Topic Sentence:	_____ Does each body paragraph have a topic sentence with a controlling idea?
Supporting Sentences:	_____ Is each paragraph about one main idea? Do your sentences support your topic sentence?
	_____ Do you have specific factual details to support what you have said?

5. **Edit your essay.**

    Work with a partner or a teacher to edit your essay. Correct spelling, punctuation, vocabulary, and grammar. Read your rough draft and try to find errors in the use of singular and plural.

    ### Example:

    Error: I would never keep <u>snake</u> as <u>pets</u>.   num
    Correct (version 1): I would never keep a snake as a pet.
    Correct (version 2): I would never keep snakes as pets.

    When you find a mistake of this type, you can mark it with the symbol "num" (number). Look at page 207 for other symbols to use when editing your work.

6. **Write your final copy.**

CHAPTER FOURTEEN

Genetically Modified (GM) Food

Pre-Reading Activity

Discuss these questions.

1. What do you look for when you are buying fruits or vegetables?
2. Why are chemicals used to grow fruits and vegetables?
3. Would you buy fruits and vegetables grown with chemicals?

Predicting

Do you know these words? Match the words with their meanings, and tell how you think each word might be connected to the topic of genetically modified food. Then compare your ideas with those in the reading.

1. ____ pesticide
2. ____ herbicide
3. ____ fertilizer
4. ____ nutritional
5. ____ drought
6. ____ hunger

a. lack of water
b. good for your diet
c. substance that kills plants
d. lack of food
e. substance that kills insects
f. substance that makes plants grow better

Genetically Modified (GM) Food

Over the past 20 years, scientists have been using technology on nature to improve food supplies. They are producing genetically modified (GM) foods by modifying, or changing, the genes of plants and animals. Genes are the codes in the cells of every living thing that determine the way they look and grow. In humans, genes determine characteristics such as the color of our eyes and how tall we are. By changing the genes of plants, scientists can cause **crops** to produce more, become **resistant** to **pests** and disease, and have more **nutritional value.** Genetically modified plants can have great benefits by increasing food supplies, protecting the environment, and even improving nutrition.

How will we feed a growing population? The world's population is expected **to exceed** 8 billion by 2025. Much of this increase will occur in the cities of **developing countries.** Unfortunately, food production, instead of increasing, has decreased over the last ten years. As it is, some 40,000 people die from hunger-related causes every day. The only way to increase food production seems to be through technology, since land and water are getting scarce. In Africa, millions of people don't have enough food to eat and are dying because drought has destroyed their food supply. If GM food crops could be developed that could resist droughts or grow in poor, dry, or salty soils, this would help poorer countries.

GM crops can protect the environment because they are kinder to nature. Many farmers today depend on chemicals such as pesticides, **herbicides,** and fertilizers to make their crops grow. Through gene biology, the genes of plants can be modified so that they will be disease-resistant and pest-resistant and still produce the same amount. The most common GM crops grown at the moment are those that resist herbicides. The second most common are those crops that kill pests. Some crops have been grown with both these genes. If a crop can resist herbicides, the farmer can spray a field with herbicides without harming the crop. All the **weeds** and other plants die, but the crop does not. By decreasing the number of weeds, the farmer increases the amount of crop grown. A good example of such a crop is GM cotton, which is often grown in the United States for cottonseed oil. If a crop can kill pests, the farmer does not have to spray so often to kill pests. An example of a pest-resistant crop is maize, which is similar to corn. There is a bacterium in the soil which produces a poison that kills insects, but it is harmless to people. Putting this bacterium gene into maize plants makes them produce their own poison, which kills the pests that eat them. This is better for the environment because it reduces the need to spray fields with pesticides and fertilizers.

Genetically modified crops may make food more nutritious by adding genes to produce more vitamins that the body needs for health and growth. For example, a kind of rice called golden rice has been genetically modified to contain vitamin A. Regular rice does not have vitamin A, and some people who live mostly on rice are missing this important vitamin. This new rice can make a big difference to those people. Modifying potatoes to contain less starch would make French fries healthier because they would not **absorb** so much fat in the cooking. GM vegetables of the future may be produced with added nutrients to help fight heart disease and cancer.

The United States grows 75 percent of the world's GM crops. More than 40 percent of the corn, 50 percent of the cotton, and 45 percent of the soybeans grown in the United States in 1999 were genetically modified. The ingredients from these crops—especially soy, which is used in many products—show up in a lot of the food we eat, from pizza, cookies, pasta, ice cream, and potato chips to soup. Are GM foods safe for our health and the environment? So far, there is no evidence that GM foods have any risks, but only time and more research will tell.

Vocabulary

Meaning

Complete each definition with one of the following words.

nutritional value	exceed	resistant
pest	scarce	herbicides
weed	crops	
absorb	developing countries	

1. A small animal or insect that harms or destroys food is a _____.

2. A wild plant that is not wanted is a _____.

3. A food that contains substances that are important for good health has _____.

4. To be greater or more than what is expected is to _____.

5. Something that is not easily found is _____.

6. To soak up or take in as a sponge takes in water is to _____.

7. Nations that are economically poor but are growing are called _____.

8. _____ kill some but not all types of plants.

9. When something has the ability to fight against something, it is _____ to it.

10. Plants such as fruit, vegetables, and grain that farmers grow are _____.

Word Building

Complete the sentences with the correct form of the word in capital letters. You may use your dictionary.

1. INSECT
   a. There are many types of _____ that can feed on crops.
   b. Farmers often use chemical _____ to protect their crops.

2. NUTRITION
   a. It is more _____ to eat food that has been grown organically.
   b. Adding vitamins can increase a food's _____ value.

3. PRODUCE
   a. GM foods can help increase food _____ in developing countries.
   b. The United States _____ 75 percent of the world's GM crops.

Comprehension

Looking for the Main Ideas

Circle the letter of the correct answer.

1. GM foods will benefit food supplies _____.
   a. around the world
   b. in Africa only
   c. in developing countries only
   d. for animals only

2. According to the reading, GM crops _____.
   a. are better for nature
   b. have herbicides
   c. give problems to farmers
   d. kill other plants

3. GM crops _____.
   a. can absorb more water
   b. are better for cooking
   c. all have vitamin A
   d. can be more nutritious

Looking for Details

Scan the reading quickly to find the answers to these questions. Write complete sentences.

1. Where will most of the increase in world population be?

   _____

   _____

2. How many people die from hunger-related causes every day?

   _____

   _____

3. What type of genetic modification to crops is the most common?

   _____

   _____

4. What is an example of this type of a GM crop?

   _____

   _____

5. How is rice genetically modified to be more nutritious?

   _____

   _____

6. How could potatoes be genetically modified?

   _____

   _____

Making Inferences and Drawing Conclusions

The answers to these questions are not directly stated in the reading. Write complete sentences.

1. How can genetically modified plants increase food production?

   _____

   _____

2. Why do you think the world population will increase mostly in cities of developing countries?

_____

_____

3. Why are land and water getting scarce?

_____

_____

4. Why are many farmers in favor of using GM foods?

_____

_____

5. Why will only time tell us if GM foods have any risks?

_____

_____

Discussion

Discuss these questions with your classmates.

1. What could the disadvantages be of GM foods?
2. Many foods in supermarkets, such as tomatoes and potatoes in the United States, are genetically modified. Would you buy GM foods? Why or why not?
3. Some animals used for food, such as salmon and pigs, can be genetically modified to grow more quickly. Do you think this is a good idea? Why or why not?

Organizing

Using Examples to Support Your Opinion

It is important to support your opinions with factual details. The more concrete your facts are, the more convincing your argument will be. Look at the following examples:

Examples:

Fact with lack of support: In some countries, the GM foods are labeled.

Concrete supporting detail: According to the Australia New Zealand Food Authority, after December 7, 2001, any GM food, either whole or an ingredient in processed food, must be labeled.

Fact with lack of support: Many people around the world are hungry.

Concrete supporting detail: According to the U.N.'s Food and Agriculture Organization (FAO) (1996), one in seven of the world's population is chronically malnourished.

In the above examples, the facts are given by the Australia New Zealand Food Authority and the U.N.'s Food and Agriculture Organization. These are the authorities. The authority should be identified by name. Vague references to authority are not acceptable in an argument. Do not use such phrases as "They say . . ." or "People say . . ." or "Authorities agree . . . ." Make the authority a reliable source. Do not use a relative or a friend as an authority.

Exercise 1

Place a check beside the statements that use reliable sources.

_____ 1.   Certain foods can be genetically modified to be better.

_____ 2. According to the journal *Nature* (vol. 419, 2002), a GM onion can be produced that will not make our eyes tear.

_____ 3. About 60 to 70 percent of packaged foods in the United States contain GM food, said Hansen, a research associate with the Consumer Policy Institute in New York (2002).

_____ 4. Europeans say that Americans eat a lot of GM foods.

_____ 5. They say that GM foods may one day harm the environment.

Remember to introduce your examples with **for example, for instance,** or **e.g.** (from Latin *exempli gratia*, meaning for example).

Writing Practice

Choose one of the following topics.
1. Write an argument in favor of or against GM plants or animals.
2. Write an argument in favor of or against organic farming.
3. Write an argument in favor of or against the use of pesticides or fertilizers.

1. Pre-writing.

Work with a partner, a group, or alone.

a. Brainstorm the topic. Choose a pre-writing brainstorming technique you prefer. (See page 208.)
b. Brainstorm for reasons either for or against the argument. Brainstorm for possible supporting details for each reason.
c. Work on a thesis statement.

2. Outlining.

a. Organize your ideas.
   Step 1: Write your thesis statement.
   Step 2: Pick the two best reasons in favor of or against the argument from your brainstorming activity.
   Step 3: Remember to begin your paragraphs with different transition words for giving reasons.
b. Make a more detailed outline. The essay outline on page 22 will help you.

3. Write a rough draft.

4. Revise your rough draft.

Using the checklist below, check your rough draft or let your partner check it.

Essay Checklist

Essay Organization

Introduction:
_____ Does it include general statements?
_____ Is there a thesis statement?

Body:
_____ Do you give relevant reasons for your argument, with a paragraph for each reason? Are your reasons identified as opinion or fact?
_____ Are different transitions used to show reasons and order?

Conclusion:
_____ Does it summarize main points or state your thesis again in other words?
_____ Is there a final comment on the topic?

Paragraph Organization

Topic Sentences:
_____ Does each body paragraph have a topic sentence with a controlling idea?

Supporting Sentences:
_____ Is each paragraph about one main idea? Do your sentences support your topic sentence?
_____ Do you have specific factual details to support what you have said?

5. Edit your essay.

Work with a partner or a teacher to edit your essay. Correct spelling, punctuation, vocabulary, and grammar. Read your draft and try to find errors that are run-on sentences.

Example:

Error: Genetically modified crops may make food more nutritious, they add genes to produce more vitamins.   *ro*

Correct: Genetically modified crops may make food more nutritious because they add genes to produce more vitamins.

When you find a mistake of this type, you can mark it with the symbol "ro" (run-on). Look at page 207 for other symbols to use when editing your work.

6. Write your final copy.

Do you know these interesting facts about animals?

Circle the letter of the best answer.

1. What does a giant panda eat?

    a. fish   b. bamboo   c. fruit   d. insects

2. How long do elephants live?

    a. 100 years   b. 60 years   c. 20 years   d. 10 years

3. Where do snow leopards live?

    a. Northern Europe   c. Central Asia
    b. South America   d. Australia

4. Which of these animals is not endangered?

    a. whale   b. zebra   c. tiger   d. frog

5. Which of these animals is extinct?

    a. mammoth   b. gorilla   c. kangaroo   d. turtle

6. What is the main cause of habitat destruction?

    a. rain   c. drought
    b. increasing size of cities   d. fires

Video Activity • Genetically Engineered Crops

1. The video is about a type of corn that was genetically modified, or genetically engineered. Why do you think this type of corn was created?

2. Review these terms used in the video: *debacle, allergen, moratorium.*

3. After you watch the video, match the terms on the left with the answers on the right. Put the correct letter on the line before each term.

    1. ____ Starlink   a. protein and possible allergen
    2. ____ EPA   b. manufacturer of GM seeds
    3. ____ CRY9C   c. Environmental Protection Agency
    4. ____ Aventis   d. where traces of Starlink were found
    5. ____ taco shells   e. GM corn that resists insects

4. Do you agree with the EPA statement that Starlink is not likely to be a health risk? Do the advantages of GM food outweigh the disadvantages?

Internet Activity

- Look up "risks of GM food" on the Internet. Then look up "benefits of GM food." What did you find out? Did your research change your opinion about GM food?

- Write a summary of your opinion and say how your research influenced your opinion.

Readings from Literature

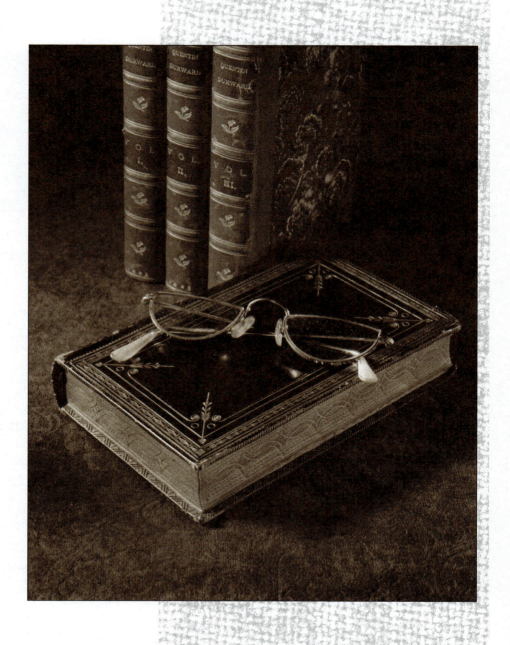

CHAPTER FIFTEEN

A Poem

Pre-Reading Activity

Discuss these questions.

1. What forms of language are in the pictures?
2. Are these languages used today?
3. What are some other languages that have died?

Predicting

Tell in what way each of the following words can be compared to language. Then compare your ideas with those in the reading.

Language is like . . .

an ocean   a volcano   a river   a mountain   a hurricane

Languages
by Carl Sandburg

1	There are no **handles** upon a language
2	**Whereby** men take hold of it
3	And mark it with signs for its remembrance.
4	It is a river, this language,
5	Once in a thousand years
6	Breaking a new **course**
7	Changing its way to the ocean.
8	It is mountain effluvia
9	Moving to **valleys**
10	And from nation to nation
11	Crossing **borders** and mixing.
12	Languages die like rivers.
13	Words **wrapped round** your tongue today
14	And broken to shape of thought
15	Between your teeth and lips speaking
16	Now and today
17	Shall be **faded hieroglyphics**
18	Ten thousand years from now.
19	Sing—and singing—remember
20	Your song dies and changes
21	And is not here to-morrow
22	Any more than the wind
23	Blowing ten thousand years ago.

Note: The word *effluvia* in line 8 refers to streams flowing down from the rainfall or melted snow.

Vocabulary

Complete each definition with one of the following words.

course	handle	fade
hieroglyphics	wrap around	whereby
valley	border	

1. _____ means by which or through which.

2. The direction of movement someone or something takes is its _____.

3. The line that divides two countries is the _____.

4. Part of something by which you can pick it up is its _____.

5. To lose color or to disappear gradually is to _____.

6. _____ are a system of writing that uses picturelike signs to represent words.

7. A _____ is the land between hills or mountains, usually with a river running through it.

8. To _____ is to encircle something.

Comprehension

Analyzing Images

Read the poem again and try to find the meaning of each of the following images.

1. "There are no handles upon a language"

    a. Languages can be difficult to learn.
    b. Languages can disappear.
    c. You cannot describe language.
    d. You cannot give language a name.

2. "It is a river, this language,
    Once in a thousand years
    Breaking a new course
    Changing its way to the ocean."

    a. Changes in language happen slowly but inevitably.
    b. Once language has changed, the change can't be reversed.
    c. Language changes are difficult to see.
    d. Language changes are unpredictable.

3. "It is mountain effluvia
    Moving to valleys
    And from nation to nation
    Crossing borders and mixing."

    a. Languages change as they cross borders.
    b. Languages do not stay within borders.
    c. Languages move slowly like mountains.
    d. Languages do not need borders to survive.

4. "Languages die like rivers."

    a. Languages are easy to forget.
    b. Languages are difficult to pronounce.
    c. Languages can be broken into pieces.
    d. Languages can dry up and be forgotten.

5. "Sing—and singing—remember
Your song dies and changes
And is not here to-morrow"

    a.   A language can change completely or disappear.

    b.   You can forget your own language easily.

    c.   A language has many melodies.

    d.   You should use your language so that it will not change.

Understanding the Poem

Read the poem again and explain each of the following images in your own words.

1.   Why is language like a river?

_____

_____

2.   Why is language like mountain effluvia?

_____

_____

3.   Why do languages die like rivers?

_____

_____

4.   Why is language like the wind?

_____

_____

Recognizing Style

Work with a partner to answer the questions.

1. What tells you that this is a poem?

   _____

   _____

2. What do you notice about the writer's use of lines and punctuation?

   _____

   _____

3. What kinds of patterns can you see in this poem?

   _____

   _____

4. Read the poem aloud. Mark the places where you would pause. Mark the words which you would say loudly or softly. Compare your answer with a partner's. Decide which reading sounds best to you.

Discussion

Discuss these questions with your classmates.
1. Why do languages die?
2. What are some languages that change from nation to nation?
3. What are some languages that have mixed with others?
4. How has your language changed? Give examples.
5. Did you enjoy reading this poem? Why or why not?

Imagery

When writers try to create a picture of something to make it seem real to us, they use imagery. To make an image or picture, they may use colorful words and expressions to make comparisons. Two kinds of imagery are the simile and the metaphor.

Simile

A *simile* compares one thing with another to show similarity. A simile uses *like* or *as*. There are many idiomatic expressions with similes, such as "as busy as a bee" and "as good as gold." Try to create your own, more interesting similes.

Example:

Languages die like rivers.

Exercise 1

Work alone, with a partner, or in a group. Complete the similes in the following sentences.

1. English spelling rules are as unreliable as _____.

2. No one speaks Latin today. Latin is as dead as _____.

3. Idioms in a language are like _____.

4. The grammar or rules of a language are as strong as _____.

5. Throughout history, language will change like _____.

Metaphor

A metaphor compares one thing with another without using *like* or *as*.

Examples:

It is a river, this language.   *(Language is compared to a river.)*

It is mountain effluvia   *(Language is compared to mountain*
Moving to valleys   *streams flowing down to valleys.)*

Work with a partner or in a group. Write metaphors to complete these sentences.

1. Language is _____.

2. Learning a language is _____.

3. Poems are the _____ of language.

Writing Practice

Read the poem again. Look back at your answers to the questions under "Understanding the Poem." Use your answers to write a paragraph explaining the metaphors and similes used in the poem in your own words. Use the sentence starters below.

The poem is about . . .
The first image is about language as a . . .
The next four lines describe how . . .
The next image describes language as . . .
Finally, language is compared to . . .

1. **Write a rough draft.**

2. **Revise your rough draft.**

   Exchange paragraphs with a classmate and ask him or her to give you comments and suggestions. Use the following questions:
   a. Are the ideas clearly expressed?
   b. Which ideas did you find most interesting and why?
   c. Give one suggestion for improving the paragraph.

3. **Edit your essay.**

   Work with a partner or teacher to edit your paragraph. Correct spelling, punctuation, vocabulary and grammar. Look at page 207 for symbols to use when editing your work.

4. **Write your final copy.**

CHAPTER SIXTEEN

A Fable

Pre-Reading Activity

Discuss these questions.

1. Why is the person in the picture not included in our society or group?

2. What are some reasons why we do not accept people into our group?

3. How is this person different from you or me?

Predicting

Look at the following words. What kind of story do you think they are from? Try to make a story using all of these words. Then compare your ideas with those in the reading.

traveler   mountain   cave   fire   outcast

A traveler, after losing his way in the mountain, **took refuge** for the night in a cave. He saw at once that another had **preceded** him and was now warming himself before a fire of sticks and leaves. When the traveler entered, the other man said, "I'm an untouchable. Be careful not to **stumble** and fall against me."

The traveler sat on the other side of the fire watching his companion. He wondered what differences made one of them an **honorable** man and the other an **outcast.** Not seeing any physical difference between them, he thought perhaps the solution **lay in another field.** He said, "Tell me, do you feel hate and joy and love, as I do? Are you capable of feeling hope and jealousy and regret?"

"Yes," said the untouchable. "I feel all those things. I also feel shame, **envy,** sorrow and pity."

And so the two men talked. They tried to discover some differences between them but did not succeed. Then the traveler said, "As far as I can see, we are very much alike," and added, "Do you know why you're an untouchable and I am not?"

"No," said the other, "I only know I was an untouchable of parents who were like myself."

There was a long silence while the two men examined each other across the fire. Finally the traveler said, "I wonder what would happen if I touched you?"

The eyes of the traveler widened at his own **audacity,** and he said, "You know—I'm going to touch you and find out." The outcast **drew back** against the wall and covered his eyes. The traveler stretched out his arms and touched the untouchable. After a time the outcast asked in a frightened voice, "Did the mountain **totter**? Did the river dry up? Did the moon fall out of the sky?"

The traveler said in astonishment, "Nothing at all happened. Everything's **precisely** as it was before."

Vocabulary

Complete each definition with one of the following words or phrases.

take refuge	precede	stumble
honorable	an outcast	lay in another field
envy	audacity	draw back
totter	precisely	

1. Someone who has the respect of others and has a good reputation is _____ .

2. To come before or happen before something else is to _____ .

3. When someone is daring and bold and perhaps rude, the person has _____ .

4. When a person is jealous of another and wants what that person has, the person has _____ .

5. A person who is not accepted or included in a group by others because of differences in such things as culture, appearance, or dress is _____ .

6. To find a place to stay that is safe from danger and discomfort is to _____ .

7. If you catch your foot on something when walking and then fall, you _____ .

8. When things are exactly the same, they are _____ as they were before.

9. To move unsteadily, as if about to fall, is to _____ .

10. To move farther away to avoid something is to _____ .

11. When the answer to something was to be found somewhere else, we can say the answer _____ .

Comprehension

Understanding the Story

Write complete answers to these questions.

1. Where does the traveler go to?

   _____

   _____

2. Who is there already?

   _____

   _____

3. What is the man doing?

   _____

   _____

4. Where does the traveler sit?

   _____

   _____

5. What kinds of feelings does the other man have?

   _____

   _____

6. What physical differences are there between the traveler and
   the man?

   _____

   _____

7. What action does the traveler take?

   _____

   _____

8. What are the consequences of this action?

   _____

   _____

Analyzing Ideas

Choose the best answer to complete the sentence.

1. The traveler went into the cave _____.
   - a. because he needed shelter
   - b. to look for a friend
   - c. because he knew of it
   - d. to find food

2. The man told the traveler, "Be careful not to stumble and fall against me" because _____.
   - a. he was afraid of getting hurt
   - b. he was an untouchable
   - c. he didn't want the traveler to get his disease
   - d. he didn't like people touching him

3. The man drew back when the traveler wanted to touch him because _____.
   - a. he thought the traveler was going to hurt him
   - b. he was scared that something bad would happen
   - c. he didn't like the traveler
   - d. people didn't usually touch him

4. After the traveler touched the other man, _____.
   - a. the traveler was angry at himself
   - b. his ideas about untouchables changed
   - c. the mountain tottered
   - d. both men's ideas about untouchables changed

Recognizing Style

Work with a partner to answer these questions.

1. Where does this story take place? What are the clues to the setting of the story? Are they specific or general? Why do you think the writer chose them?

   _____

   _____

2. "Did the mountain totter? Did the river dry up? Did the moon fall out of the sky?" Describe the tone of these questions. What effect do they have?

   _____

   _____

3. How does the writer's opinion differ from the opinion of the characters in the story? How does the writer convey his opinion? Is the writer's style effective? Why or why not?

   _____

   _____

4. In this story, the characters are used to represent abstract ideas. What ideas do they represent?

   _____

   _____

Discussion

Discuss these questions with your classmates.

1. How do the men feel about the word *untouchable* at the beginning of the story and how do they feel about it at the end?
2. Why do people give names like *enemy, outcast,* and *untouchable* to each other?
3. How do we feel about the people we give these names to?
4. How could this story take place in today's society?
5. What can we do to overcome these kinds of feelings?

Writing Practice

Think of a type of person who is sometimes not accepted by a group because of sex, dress, customs, etc. Write a story similar to this fable with different characters and a present-day setting. Before you start writing, make notes about each of the following:

- Who are the characters?
- What is the setting?
- What do the characters learn by the end of the story?
- What will the reader find out at the end?
- What is the main message of the story?

1. Write a rough draft.

2. Revise your rough draft.

   Exchange stories with a classmate and ask him or her to give you comments and suggestions. Use the following questions.

   a. Are the ideas clearly expressed?
   b. Which ideas did you find most interesting and why?
   c. Give one suggestion for improving the story.

3. Edit your essay.

   Work with a partner or teacher to edit your story. Correct spelling, punctuation, vocabulary, and grammar. Look at page 207 for symbols to use when editing your work.

4. Write your final copy.